# Frontier and Metropolis

# Frontier and Metropolis: Regions, Cities, and Identities in Canada before 1914

The
Donald G. Creighton Lectures
1987

## J.M.S. CARELESS

UNIVERSITY OF TORONTO PRESS
Toronto Buffalo London

© University of Toronto Press 1989
Toronto  Buffalo  London
Printed in Canada

ISBN 0-8020-5824-8

Printed on acid-free paper

Canadian Cataloguing in Publication Data

Careless, J.M.S., 1919–
Frontier and metropolis

(The Donald G. Creighton lectures ; 1987)
ISBN 0-8020-5824-8

1. Metropolitan areas – Canada – History.
2. Regionalism – Canada – History.
3. Canada – History. I. Title. II. Series.

HT127.C37  1989      307.7'6'0971      C89-093221-2

# Contents

# Foreword

**D**ONALD G. CREIGHTON was born in 1902 and died in 1979. The son of a Methodist minister, and the grandson of a feminist, Donald Creighton rose, via Victoria College, Balliol College, Oxford, and the Department of History at this University to the top of his profession. He joined the Department of History at the University of Toronto in 1927 and retired, forty-four years later, as a University Professor, the highest honour this institution can bestow on its faculty. He served a five-year stint as head of the department in the late fifties – no chairman, let alone genderless chair was he, and during this period he also served a term as president of the Canadian Historical Association.

Donald Creighton was hired by the History Department six years after the Department of Political Economy had hired Harold Innis. In his first ten years as an academic, Donald Creighton wrote only two short articles. But then came his first great work, *The Commercial Empire of the St Lawrence*, published in 1937, a work that was clearly influenced by the same forces that were evident in the books and articles which Innis had published during the previous ten years. Innis, as is well known, had developed the theory that Canada's political development had resulted naturally from its essential geographical features, whose principal one he labelled, inelegantly, the 'drainage system.' In 1937, Innis's 'drainage system' became Creighton's 'empire of the St Lawrence.' There then followed over thirty extraordinarily fruitful years in which Donald Creighton articulated a grand vision of Canadian history in which the characters he so brilliantly depicted interacted with the circumstances that his friend Innis had so starkly delineated. In the twenty years following 1937 there appeared *British North America at Confederation, Dominion of the North*, the two-volume biography of Sir John A. Macdonald, his biography of Innis and his *Story of Canada*. This remarkable output was recognized in an endless stream of awards and prizes. The writing of Canadian history from 1935 until the early sixties was dominated by the man that this series of lectures is designed to honour, and the identifying marks of this history were its literary elegance and its national vision.

On Donald Creighton's death in 1979, a fund was established to create a special lectureship in his memory, and the lectures that comprise this volume were the second in the series. The first Creighton lectures, *Polyethnicity and National Unity in World History*, by William H. McNeill, were delivered in 1985 and published in 1986.

The second Creighton lecturer was born as the sixteen-year-old Creighton was completing high school. In many respects, Maurice Careless's career replicates that of Donald Creighton. Maurice too went to the University of Toronto, graduating with a BA in history in 1940. He proceeded to Harvard the following year and received his master's degree, and, in 1950, his doctorate. He worked in the Department of External Affairs during the war and commenced his academic career in the Department of History at the University of Toronto in 1945. He progressed rapidly through the ranks until 1959 when, at the age of 40, he succeeded Donald Creighton as chairman, a position he held for eight years. In 1977, like Creighton before him, he became University Professor; he retained that position until he retired in 1984. Also emulating his distinguished predecessor, Maurice Careless has won numerous awards.

While Maurice Careless's career followed that of Donald Creighton closely, his vision of Canadian history has been distinctly different. Whereas Creighton's great biography was of the Conservative Father of Confederation, Sir John A. Macdonald, Maurice Careless based his historical career on his two-volume biography of the Clear Grit Liberal leader, George Brown, editor of the Toronto *Globe* from 1844 until 1880. Beginning with this reinterpretation of Brown's role in the politics of Confederation, Maurice Careless has, for thirty-five years, developed a 'metropolitan' analysis of Canadian history that is strikingly at variance with the national perspective of Creighton. Maurice Careless has in his own books and articles and, just as importantly, in the thirty or so doctoral theses he has supervised, stressed the regional character of Canada and the crucial role the development of metropolitan areas played in Canadian history.

Donald Creighton may not have agreed with Maurice Careless's approach to Canadian history, but he would have been impressed by the masterful synthesis that follows.

Michael G. Finlayson
Chair, Department of History
University of Toronto
September 1988

# Preface

Tｈｅｓｅ lectures, presented through the Donald Creighton Foundation at the Department of History of the University of Toronto, represent an effort to condense my own past years of study on metropolitan relations in Canada. They seek to make some fairly brief, broad statements about the powerful interplay between metropolis and hinterland, dominant city and supporting region, during the founding eras of this country before the First World War. I was deeply gratified to have been named Donald Creighton Lecturer in 1987, and in that prized role to have had the opportunity of delivering my views on the 'metropolitan approach' to Canadian urban and regional history. I earnestly hope that the lectures which follow will illustrate and illuminate that approach across more than four centuries. At this moment I would only want to add that, on the regional or hinterland side, the huge territories of an ultimate Canadian transcontinental union long remained thinly occupied frontier reaches; and so 'frontier' must necessarily be coupled with 'metropolis' (the focal point of dominating power) through much of Canada's experience to 1914 – or in its north, even till today.

The basic terms and concepts which I have thus employed are also considered in the four lectures below. In regard to these discourses, it should be noted, however, that while I gave the first three in the Creighton series at Toronto, the last has been appended here at the suggestion of the University of Toronto Press to round out the set of offerings. This fourth lecture was originally delivered in somewhat different form at the University of Victoria. But when revised to fit in suitably with the other three, it did seem to supply an effective complement to the comprehensive sweep which I was attempting to extend over the opening ages of Canadian history.

Two more concerns call for remark: first, that I myself am considerably conscious of omissions or the need for detailed qualifications in my inevitably generalized lecture accounts. All too possibly, specific errors may lie embedded in such general treatments; but one has to launch out somewhere, or else stay uselessly safe in non-pronouncement. My belief continues to hold that overall historical statements are vitally required, even if they may well contain particular flaws themselves. The second topic is far happier. As Creighton Lecturer I want cordially to acknowledge the hospitality, kindness, and comradeship received from the Department of History at the University of Toronto – my old department – and especially received from Professor Michael Finlayson in its presiding chair. For me, my time in the lectureship was a treasured homecoming. Yet, beyond that, I want most warmly to thank the Creighton Foundation and assuredly the members of the Creighton family who made my tenancy as lecturer not only congenial, but thoroughly enjoyable as well.

JMSC

# LECTURE ONE

## Matters of Structure and Perception

# Matters of
# Structure and
# Perception

I COULD NOT FEEL more
pleased and honoured to be this year's Creighton Lecturer. I knew Donald Creighton for more than four
decades; in the late 1930s as one of my tutors and
professors at the University of Toronto, and after 1945 as
my close colleague and valued mentor in the University's Department of History. His high scholarly
achievements, commemorated in the lectures given
under the distinguished auspices of the Creighton
Foundation, scarcely need further tribute from me; but
I should, I must, record the personal intellectual debt I
owe him. My own discourses here do not presume to
pay it off. Still, they do represent a sincere acknowledg-
ment of an indebtedness that has many aspects, of
which I would like to mention three.

First, there was so much that I received as a student
from Donald Creighton's teaching, as stimulating in

small tutorial groups as it was engrossing in big lecture classes. I think back to his vivid lectures on the French Revolution or the lively tutorials I took with him on Tudor England, long before I arrived at the closer interests of Canadian history. Whatever the subject, he lit it with his energy and enthusiasm. But, second, he furnished teaching of another sort through his paramount abilities as an author. One could not but be affected by the masterly Creightonian writing in volumes that provided veritable models for Canadian history as literature – which it has to be, unless we are ready to leave the computers to flash blips of data at one another. I well remember how in the 1950s Donald would inveigh against that insipid catch-all category in the annual Governor General's Literary Awards, 'academic non-fiction,' which included history. As he said, that implied books which were too academic to be readable and too non-fictional to be creative. His own works, instead, left clear impressions of what Canadian history could be: eminently readable and evocative, marked both by creative imagination and carefully documented scholarship, a compelling blend quite beyond the talent of a multitude of make-it-all-up novelists.

But what left most impression on my mind was the distinct and particular sort of national meaning which Donald Creighton gave to Canadian history. To me, it seemed that before him writings on Canada's past had largely illustrated the adaptation of British political institutions to an emerging country overseas, or had essentially demonstrated the northward reach of American social realities unchecked by the international boundary, or had mainly expressed the economic workings of a world staple-trades area. All these perspectives, whether they reached me at Toronto from Chester

Martin, Frank Underhill, or Harold Innis, had their different kinds of validity, and each would certainly influence my thinking. Yet it was Donald Creighton who brought fresh context and significance to Canadian history; from within the country, so to speak. He deeply sensed the promises and penalties of the land mass, the play of weighty collective interests, and the sweeping pressures from an adjoining United States which had always to be met. But, equally, he saw the role of the wills and capacities of individuals bound up with Canada, thus forming historic conjunctions of 'character and circumstance,' as he would succinctly phrase it.

It is hardly news that Creighton's interpretation of Canadian history was that of a nationalist, an unabashed nationalist – or seldom abashed, at any rate. His conception, of course, was built about the great St Lawrence trade and traffic route: Canada's own long east-west axis, which first underlay the Montreal fur empire and then the transcontinental dominion of John A. Macdonald, yet which was nevertheless threatened continually by the north-south pulls of continentalism (for which read American takeover). This 'Laurentian' construct was hence a kind of historical declaration of independence, notably against the United States; but not simply so. It was also a projection, or a presumption, of a distinctive Canadian historic identity proceeding on its own national course of development. Now obviously nationalism in Canada has known various shifts and phases. Tariff nationalists who were once John A's Tory tycoons today may be Bob White's labour unionists. Politicians urging continental camaraderie are no longer Laurier liberals but Mulroney Conservatives. With changing currents such as these, a nationalist conception of Canadian history like

Creighton's Laurentianism is not likely to stay in lasting favour or even to go uncriticized; and I would not endorse it all myself. Nonetheless, much remains outside contention. The Laurentian approach did have a widespread appeal, one that reflected far more than its gifted promoter's literary talents, for it evinced keen insight and struck responsive chords. In brief, it offered a positive, at times ardent, assessment of historical Canadian experience – not at all in the customary Canadian vein of self-disparagement. And to doubters or detractors Creighton made forceful, even withering, reply. He was surpassing in the verve he brought to Canadian history. The national distinction he gave it was very much his own.

All this seems plentiful reason for feeling indebted. I would like to think, however, that I can move onward from Donald Creighton's work – recognizing its strong value without adopting it *in toto* – as I seek to present a further and by no means unrelated approach to Canada's development. This approach agrees with his root position that Canadian history, whatever its affinities, does have distinctive national qualities and yields inherent interpretations of its own. The lectures to follow will try in their own way to sustain that stand.

As to their theme, in the largest sense they deal with the relations of cities and regions in Canada, from the initial rise of European occupation on the Atlantic coasts to the filling in of the West before the world war of 1914–18. More specifically, they concern the connections between a most prominent and powerful kind of city, the metropolis, and those broad segments of Canadian territory which grew from raw frontiers into populated and developed regions. 'Frontier' and 'region' are terms that run through much of Canadian history. So should the term 'metropolis,' the power centre associated with a great deal of frontier and regional growth. Without doubt, I have been saying this sort of thing for longer than I might like to admit. It is over thirty years since I first published an article on frontierism and metropolitanism in Canadian history. All the same, I dare to venture forth once more: because the ties between the metropolis and its supporting/dependent territory – its hinterland in region or frontier – appear so pervasive and influential, and no less because those ties can have an important bearing on the emergence of patterns in Canadian identity. In my view, national, regional, and perhaps some other forms of identity in Canada show vital links with metropolitan-hinterland relationships across both time and space. That is, accordingly, the line which this set of lectures will trace out.

This first one, 'Matters of Structure and Perception,' presents an overall appraisal of the historical connections between metropolitan centres and frontiers or regions in Canada, connections which were both structural and perceptual in kind. That is, they might be displayed not only in economic structures, political fabrics, or social networks, but also in attitudes of regard, modes of opinion, or popular images and traditions – all, in turn, to affect identity. I will not try to spell out now what will be examined later. Suffice it to observe that metropolitan and hinterland communities were conjoined through mental and habitual appreciations as well as through physical operations and organizations. My opening lecture will thus pay heed to these varied sorts of attributes, as it discusses the functioning of metropolis and hinterland, frontier and region across the country down to 1914. The second lecture will inquire into some major conceptual treatments given to frontier and metropolis in history, to conclude, naturally, with my own preferred versions of frontierism and metropolitanism. And the third will seek to evaluate the impact of metropolitanism on distinctive features of Canada's identity that are revealed in its historical experience. A fourth and final discourse will then apply this assembled structure (properly coupled with perceptions) to the founding stages of Canadian growth; that is, to eras reaching into the early nineteenth century.

I hope that the complete set may add something to the comprehension of general Canadian history, both in its national context and its international relevance. But note the reference to 'general' history; I did not say 'urban' or 'regional.' For my theme is not wholly urban: it largely omits the internal developments in cities to concentrate on their external relations. As for regional activities, it also leaves many aside in order to fix mainly on dealings between the region and the city/metropolis. At the same time, all four lectures look broadly and continually to urban or regional considerations, as they pursue their chosen approach to a sizeable part of Canada's past. And so at last to the topics of our initial lecture, starting, all but inevitably, with the frontier beginnings of this country.

2

It is a truism – if no less true – that Canada took shape through the successive occupation of frontiers, the forward margins of an acquisitive society reaching out to fresh areas of resources. When sixteenth-century Europe advanced a fishing frontier to the northeastern coasts of North America, a process began which eventually brought the whole Canadian land mass and its indigenous peoples into recorded history. In following periods European migrants and their descendants invaded one great resource region after another with frontiers of fishing, fur trading, or lumbering, of farming, ranching, or mining. By the early twentieth century extending frontier growth had spanned the west to the Pacific and implanted populous regional communities that transformed the realms of the relatively sparse native inhabitants. Huge areas to the north remained still barely penetrated by the new societies at the onset of the First World War. Nevertheless, by then a Canadian transcontinental state had form and content from coast to coast, binding internal linkages, and a well-organized rural and urban life. While northward advances and intensive growth would obviously continue, by 1914 frontier expansion had already marked out the present Canadian entity and, more particularly, set structures and perceptions of both regional and national identity within its bounds.

Yet behind this striking process of expansion lay the impelling, directing power of cities; above all, of the metropolis, the pre-eminent urban place. As a prime focus of trade, wealth, leadership, and enterprise, the metropolis could effectively dominate wide economic hinterlands, whether in territories adjacent or lying far remote. Moreover, the policy decisions, the stores of knowledge, and the techniques that were concentrated in such a commanding city were transmitted outward to the hinterland, working to organize it not in economic terms alone, but in political and social systems, cultural institutions, and built environments as well. In older countries, long-established hinterlands commonly contained many lesser urban places; places, that is, distinguished not only by their concentration of people at particular sites, but also by economic functions and social patterns differentiated from those of the surrounding countryside. And these lesser cities and towns in turn were linked with and subordinated to dominant metropolitan centres. In countries still undergoing major processes of settlement, like Canada before the First World War, hinterlands generally stretched to near-empty margins which at first held only small supply bases, the merest urban outposts, within their sweep. But these outposts, too, were tied to distant metropolitan dynamism, as were the frontier margins themselves. In fact, frontier expansion to a high degree expressed the thrust of the metropolis for more resources and trading hinterlands. This insistent drive, by no means ending in 1914, did a great deal to mould the settled regions and Canadian identities apparent by that date.

In a newly entered Canada, metropolitan power was initially exerted from outside. From the turn of the seventeenth century, core communities in western Europe, embodied especially in the capital cities of Paris and London, reached across the Atlantic to plant enduring bases, garrisons, or entrepôts on the frontiers of commerce and resources that were spreading into eastern North America. Principal frontier bases such as Quebec (1608), Montreal (1642), and subsequently Halifax (1749) gradually rose to be influential urban centres in themselves as their own trade hinterlands developed. They gained positions of internal headship beneath the external metropolitan dominance. The surrender of New France in 1760 (confirmed by the peace treaty of 1763) removed the power of Paris and left London's hegemony supreme; but within it the Canadian centres built up their own domains. Indeed, by the close of the eighteenth century, that of fur-trading Montreal had reached the Pacific. Then, on through the nineteenth century into the twentieth, still other internal centres built sizeable headships over freshly growing hinterlands, in time rising to the stature of regional metropolises: most notably, Toronto, from about the 1850s, Winnipeg and Vancouver from around the 1890s. By 1914, as well, two cities had broadly achieved significance and scope as national-scale metropolises: long-leading, top-ranking Montreal and, more recently, Toronto become a fast-advancing contender. By this time Ottawa, too, might be termed a national political metropolis, as the ruling seat of federal authority since 1867.

Other enlarging cities secured ascendancy in more restricted regional areas; among them, St John's and Saint John, Hamilton and London, Regina, Edmonton, and Victoria. An urban metropolitan hierarchy developed within Canada, though its structure was never neatly ordered or delimited, but featured overlapping hinterlands and many areas of rivalry. Meanwhile, major metropolises below the American border made strong connections with Canadian territories: from Boston and New York long before 1850 to Chicago and San Francisco thereafter. Nor had London's transatlantic sway lost its effect by 1914. Consequently, the whole expansive growth of Canada was played upon by metropolitan forces, external or internal; and no frontier, however remote or thinly held, lay beyond their influences. Frontier and metropolis were interlinked persistently, whatever their changing circumstances.

Canadian frontiers might all in truth be seen as the farthest, thinnest, hinterlands of dominant cities. In the course of time these outlying margins usually built up their own resident populations and developed growing societies with their own town-and-country structure, characteristic pursuits, and collective interests, while still newer margins pushed beyond them. In other words, frontiers might assuredly become maturing regions, where, as in the Plains West, a locally leading town like Winnipeg could itself grow into a regionally ascendant metropolitan city. Yet from rudimentary, scantily occupied frontier to well-organized and populated region, the metropolitan-hinterland relationship prevailed. As one illustration, the Upper Canada farm frontier of the earlier nineteenth century developed into a thickly inhabited, prosperous Southern Ontario region; but Toronto's command over this hinterland only increased, as the pioneer farming phase was succeeded by the day of railways, multiplying towns, and factory industries. The basic point is that frontiers amount to cases, or stages, within the enduring association of metropolis and hinterland, which at its fullest range could cover opening margins, coalescing regions, and the firmly set societies of older countrysides and towns.

The comprehensive metropolitan-hinterland association, wholly evident in Canada to 1914, was not in itself an equal partnership. The very power of city dominance makes that plain. Hinterland societies assuredly might come to perceive their lot as one of subservience and exploitation, as pawns of high-powered city interests, and they recurrently expressed this view in frontier and regional protest movements. Furthermore, metropolitan power groups might well prove imperious and self-seeking, not to say arrogant and grasping. Still further, metropolitan exploitation of hinterland resources – a darker label for development – could lead to their depletion or exhaustion, although that was as likely to occur at the hands of local residents as at the behest of city overlords. Too frequently, the results of such a ravaging march of progress were despoiled farmlands, cut-over forest replaced by scrawny bush, or abandoned mines and settlements. Frontier reaches did not always rise to fruitful countrysides and flourishing towns; they could stagnate, even degenerate, instead. Most did effectively mature; but whether they swelled or declined, the sterner costs along the way fell on the hinterland populace, not the urban command centre. For if the main, directing dynamism in development lay with the chief decision-making cities, so they also collected much more of the concentrated profits than the distributed losses. Popular images of the ruthless big city and the victimized countryside reflected the plain perceptions of inequity.

Nonetheless, while the metropolitan-hinterland relationship was not necessarily equitable, it was inherently complementary because each side needed and used the other. The metropolitan centre obtained the primary resources, the staple commodities in fur and foodstuffs, mine or forest products, which Canadian hinterlands provided; and it increasingly gained valuable markets there for the manufactures and other goods it offered. On the other side, the hinterlands of Canada drew as clearly on the metropolis for the investment, organization, transport, and technology required to bring yields from their raw resources. Supplies and capital, people and skills, flowed out to them. As young frontier societies thus grew, their needs grew correspondingly. And as supply-and-service towns appeared in the rising regions, they were linked in networks reaching back to metropolitan sources of manifold goods, credit, and expertise. Advancing regional communities continually had to look to dominant central places for directives that deeply affected their own activities, whether issuing from banks and merchant houses, transport corporations, or large manufacturing plants – each of which in its turn looked to hinterland outlets or inputs. Other kinds of networks also integrated the two sides: fabrics of law courts and administrative or religious authorities, press and publication services, professional, educational, and cultural facilities, all largely centred in leading cities but all radiating to the territories beyond. Consequently, in spite of the many divergences and discords that could appear between hinterland and metropolis, the two were not dichotomously exclusive or opposed but were essentially tied in with one another, functioning through mutual interaction.

Newly opening frontier hinterlands were decidedly tied in, notwithstanding their seeming isolation and the stark contrasts of life there with that of the metropolis. They really held few free agents whose backs were stoutly turned against the world outside in spite of common myths of pioneer self-reliance and forest-born independence. There were, no doubt, the get-rich transients, the wilderness seekers, the indifferent, or the incapable. But the majority of Canadian pioneers sought to re-create their old world as fast as possible (though with more room and opportunity), looking to that world and remaining dependent on it in quite basic ways. Security and order on nascent Canadian frontiers widely rested on structures provided and maintained from outside, as evidenced by military garrisons in the Great Lakes woodlands or North-West

Mounted Police posts on the open plains. The very people who took up the forward margins often came there through outside direction and provision. In seventeenth-century New France, settlers were channelled to the St Lawrence by a metropolitan bureaucracy in Paris; in eighteenth-century Nova Scotia, they were shipped by London officialdom to found Halifax; while in the nineteenth-century west they occupied prairie lands laid out under the political authority of Ottawa and made accessible by the Canadian Pacific Railway (CPR), which the transport enterprises of Montreal had constructed. Of course personal initiatives and unarranged migrations were much involved as well; but from early colonial land grants to CPR land sales, frontier ventures vitally relied on metropolitan auspices. And the venturers could seldom escape the power that distant metropolitan interests might wield over their success or failure.

In fact, settlers in Canada's frontier hinterlands were decidedly economic dependents and displayed little of the self-subsistence which popular belief has frequently assigned to them. Atlantic outport fishermen, Quebec timber hewers, prairie homesteaders, and mountain miners all served distant markets and counted heavily on goods or equipment brought in from outside. Perhaps the forest fur trader was the most self-subsistent frontiersman; yet he, too, depended on imported trade goods, traps, and guns, and on the demands for furs in the metropolis. In these respects he was practically a metropolitan outrunner in the primeval forest. And notwithstanding the capacity for innovation and resourceful change long credited to the pioneer, settlers in Canada, however much they may have done to adapt successfully to hard new physical environments (often learning from the native Indians), kept, overall, much more to the views and practices of their parent societies. Thus, they habitually transferred political traditions, cultural images, and social norms; and while these were adjusted to different settings, influences from the older world beyond went right on affecting them. In sum, frontier peripheries were remote but not at all cut off, intrinsically aspiring but no less tributary. From the start they were bound in need and outlook to metropolitan cores: bound by structure and perception both.

Hence, even in earliest frontier Canada the metropolis loomed large: the larger, one might say, because there then were so few intervening urban places between the outside centres of dominance and the newly emerging hinterlands. In later times, when internal metropolises, regional cities, and a host of minor towns had appeared, the metropolitan-hinterland linkages grew vastly more complex. But they still operated and could be witnessed all across the country, not least on the latest frontiers to open before 1914. The interplay between metropolis and frontier, city and region, was present and significant throughout.

3

The reciprocal, far-reaching relationship of metropolis and hinterland had still a further significance: for the shaping of patterns of identity in the settled hinterland regions that grew from Canadian frontiers. My use of 'identity' here refers to those bonding structures and perceptions, which came to mark – or identify – the major regional communities that formed in Canada. In this regard, their ethnic and geographic attributes particularly deserve attention because to a large extent each region derived historically from its own distinctive combination of entering peoples and territorial geography. To treat ethnic features first, regional societies developing in Canada before 1914 as virtually new growths in recently occupied terrain were clearly much affected by the principal human groups and heritages transmitted to them during their formative years. It is evident, as well, that metropolitan agencies of transmission did a good deal to implant social and cultural traits of identity in rising Canadian regions.

The characterizing effect of ethnic transfer is very apparent in the case of the French stock, language, and culture lastingly conveyed to the St Lawrence Valley before the British conquest by the power of imperial France. Yet provinces colonized by Britain which arose in other areas displayed their own identifying ethnic patterns, predominantly Anglo-Celtic in origin. In a Nova Scotia from which most French Acadians had been expelled in 1755 by British imperial force, New England planters and American Loyalists – local migrants – were joined from the late eighteenth century on by numerous transatlantic arrivals from Scotland; in a Newfoundland basically settled from seventeenth-century England and eighteenth-century Ireland, Scots and American colonials remained few; while Prince Edward Island and New Brunswick acquired their own particular blends of these principal Atlantic region stocks. Toward the centre, beyond a mainly francophone Quebec, anglophone Ontario had by the mid-nineteenth century received its own prime founding elements or 'charter groups': an initial Loyalist vanguard after the American Revolution, followed by transborder spillovers of American land-seekers; but, above all, flows of Irish, English, and Scots direct from the United Kingdom, then the metropolitan heartland of a world empire. The western plains frontiers were filled in from the later nineteenth century by another largely anglophone amalgam, which soon became increasingly infused with non-English-speaking settlers from continental Europe, to produce a noteworthy ethnic diversity not equalled in other Canadian regions down to 1914. By that date the far western mountains and Pacific shores had developed still another British, Canadian, and American mix of occupants, with some minor non-anglophone ingredients, including Asian. Altogether, the regional societies that appeared were differently and distinctly marked by the major population groups transmitted to them – ethnic contributions to identity.

In the principal transfers of people and their inheritances to emerging hinterlands, timing, too, could play an effective part. The charter settlers of the St Lawrence Valley frontier brought from their authoritative French homeland the classic institutions, precepts, and images of the *ancien régime* under Louis XIV. The British emigrants who flowed into Ontario moved from a metropolitan Britain caught up in Victorian industrial expansion, widening vistas of political reform, and triumphant laissez-faire liberalism. Western settlement mostly took place within still another milieu, that of transcontinental railway undertakings from the 1880s, of massing corporate capitalism and countering efforts at collective social action. These vital times of foundation affected the modes of outlook or perceptions in each regional society, and through each period the links back to metropolitan sources of ideas and models stayed fully apparent.

Meanwhile, as the newly settled societies burgeoned, the aboriginal populations within their bounds were critically disrupted, then essentially excluded. Comparatively scattered, increasingly outnumbered, the native peoples were shifted to reserves or left to the fringes of settlement and the wilderness expanses still beyond. They found little place in the swelling regional communities themselves, thanks considerably to the white ethnocentricism which the entering migrants so often brought with them from their homeland core communities. Out of sight, out of mind: that was the virtual 'solution to the native problem,' as European settlement took over unrestrained.

Throughout the whole course of occupation, metropolitan-based agencies were continually involved in transmitting settlers and their cultural baggage to frontier and regional hinterlands. These forwarding instruments appeared in the long lines of sail and later steam transport that moved emigrants over the Atlantic to Canadian coasts and waterways, and in the major rail systems which subsequently took them on by land, threading across the continent. From the Napoleonic era to the mid-Victorian, ships in the square-timber trade that served metropolitan Britain sailed outbound in ballast to colonial ports, thus affording cheap passage to masses of poor settlers from the British Isles – living ballast in their cavernous holds. During the early twentieth century, transatlantic steamship companies (and Canadian immigration and railway agents) mounted efforts on the European mainland to draw fresh masses into the settlement traffic by sea. To a continuing outflow from Britain they added Slavic and Germanic streams that fed Canadian cities, northern lumber camps and mines, or western farms – along with Italians, Jews, Hungarians, Scandinavians, and still other elements. Onward to 1914 – on, indeed, to the present – directing metropolitan instruments of many kinds built up the ethnic structure of Canada's hinterlands, further to affect their various regional identities.

This is in no way to assume that factors intrinsic to the hinterlands – above all, the forces of geography – did not shape these identities as well. Climate, natural barriers and lines of access, water systems, soil and resources distributions set fundamental terms for the human communities growing inside these territories, guiding initial frontier penetrations, mapping out principal areas for occupation, prefiguring staple regional activities and, in time, urban and industrial locations as well. Each town or ultimate metropolitan city was itself constantly affected by the advantages and limitations of its particular site. And because metropolitan-hinterland relations operated across space, they, too, were comprised within frameworks of geography. Frontier and regional development in Canada everywhere reflected the profound influence of physical environments.

In an Atlantic area of deeply indented coasts, ready approach by sea, and abundant fishing resources, distinct maritime societies developed from the fishermen's harbours of the sixteenth and seventeenth centuries: edging a rugged terrain that held only limited farmland, but in time exploiting its often thick timber cover. On the vital continental entry of the St Lawrence, the Canadiens of New France/Quebec spread farms and commerce along that strategic waterway well before 1700 and reached up such chief tributaries as the Saguenay or the Ottawa to vast forest domains beyond. Starting in the 1790s, Ontario grew prosperous and populous in the fertile lowlands of moderate climate that stretched southwest from the St Lawrence Valley into the heart of the Great Lakes basin: a long belt of well-endowed terrain which was backed to northward by the lumber and mining potentialities of the rugged Precambrian Shield and which had access all along its front to the grand inland waterway of the Upper St Lawrence and the Lakes. The sweeping interior plains to westward – an immensity of open prairie, parkland, and northern forest – were more arduous in climate but rich in soils for cereal culture, paramountly attracting grain growers who arrived from the 1870s on, first in trickles, then in waves. And the soaring, massed Cordilleran ranges of the far west set the most telling terms of all to access or occupation. Yet river courses wound through the enormous barriers, foothills and intermontane plateaus offered ranching and sheltered valleys farming, while the giant forests of humid Pacific slopes provided plentiful lumbering. Still further, the mineral wealth stored in the western ranges, first tapped by prospectors panning for alluvial gold up the Fraser River in 1858, invited hard-rock mining by the 1890s within the mountain piles themselves. In this formidable setting, the mix of constraints and opportunities derived from physical features most plainly characterized the course of hinterland development. But that was innately true in all of the five main historical regions that emerged in Canada: the Atlantic area, Quebec, Ontario, the Plains West, and the Far West. Their geography stamped them.

It is imperative to note, however, that these were indeed historical regions. They were not necessarily, or even mostly, co-terminous with natural regions, but emerged in history – with limits and divisions of their own. A natural region can be defined by its physical aspects; a historical region displays the interaction of human and geographic elements over time. This latter description properly fits the chief populated territorial segments of Canada, in full evidence before 1914. Accordingly, the Atlantic region showed common natural attributes, but also the separate experience of the four provinces that shared it. (Newfoundland, among them, was not even to join Canada politically until 1949). Subdivision would mark the Plains West also, where Manitoba, Saskatchewan, and Alberta expressed their own variants of regional history and interests. And while the mountainous Far West was chiefly to be identified with one province, British Columbia, the natural region itself ran on northward through the Yukon Territory. Physical and historical limits were not equivalent; above all, in the two big central entities, Quebec and Ontario.

These, in fact, were very much historical constructions, erected as provinces in their own right. Both were based in the St Lawrence–Great Lakes agricultural lowlands which really form one geographic unit. But history split it between two societies of settlement, the one predominantly French by lineage and culture, the other Anglo-American with British institutional forms. Then each spread out onto the Shield, that huge mass of ancient rock sprawled across the Canadian mid-north from Labrador to the western sub-Arctic: a decidedly different natural region from the Quebec and Ontario lowlands, uninviting to land settlement, if beckoning in natural resources. Hence Ontario and Quebec, while always engaged with geography, were not physical unities. They were human, historical creations – veritable provincial empires – though no less real for that. The prairie provinces of the Plains West came to transcend natural bounds as well. Manitoba and Sas-

katchewan included large areas of Shield country;
Alberta a mountain belt rising from the foothills of the
Rockies to the continental divide; and British Columbia
held a part of the plains in its northeastern inland
stretches.

One might well wonder if it is worth dealing with
regions at all, or better just to keep to specific provincial
units – but that would be over-reacting. Undoubtedly as
far as frontier beginnings were concerned, historical
regions, by and large, antedated subsequent provincial
jurisdictions. More important, they constituted the
main underlying frames within which Canada grew.
Most important, there were within these frames strong
historical affinities which identified an Atlantic regional community overall as well as a Plains Western or
Far Western collectivity, or a Quebec or Ontario society.
To put it most generally, Canada did produce a major
set of regional entities which Canadians perceived as
such and still find present now. And the fact remains, in
any case, that geography alone did not determine the
five main historic regions, whatever its effects might be
within each of them.

In truth, occupying populations structured new
social environments within the physical settings. Canada's main historic sections developed both from within
and without, through people acting on their natural
surroundings and being acted upon in return as incho-
ate frontiers rose into well-defined regions. Physical
factors thus interfused with human – with ethnocul-
ture, metropolitan input, economic effort, and political
organization – to delineate regionalism, which is to say,
the community fabric and group consciousness that
mark historical regions. Their man-made properties
appeared in rural landscapes, resource workplaces,
and urban locales, but equally in characteristic mind-

sets and behaviour. Material aspects of regionalism were displayed by shingled Atlantic fishing villages, by Quebec's seigneurial strip fields and Catholic churches derived from the French baroque, by Ontario's substantial farmsteads or Victorian British town halls, and by prairie grain-elevator hamlets or west coast logging camps. The immaterial aspects of regionalism were revealed in the collective sense of common qualities of life and interests that developed within each broad territory, though powerfully influenced in all by physical conditions.

For instance, grain farmers on the western plains grew keenly, jointly, aware of the vagaries of a climate that might bring plentiful harvests one year, ruinous drought or frost another. They forged a common identity in battles against natural threats, while prairie distances and remoteness from markets further heightened regional awareness among these widely scattered producers. Elsewhere, stark mountain vastness, the press of northern rock and forest, somewhat idealized vistas of rural environments in Quebec or Ontario, or the stress of life on hard Atlantic coasts evoked other broad regional perceptions and attitudes. They were increasingly evinced in environment and social conduct, and in traditions, writings, and political opinions. These distinctive stances would share amply in fixing regional identities within the outlines of a Canadian nation-state.

4

Yet metropolitan factors took an ample share as well – and not only by operating on a hinterland region from outside which is largely what has been observed of them so far. They could operate *inside* the region also, being in no way merely extrinsic to its growth. From frontier times onward, metropolitan organization was, in fact, a basic part of an area's own internal urban development. And the regionally dominant cities that ultimately resulted, their centring of regional structure and perceptions about themselves, proved highly consequential for the patterning of identity.

In economic terms, the young towns that appeared along an emerging region's traffic routes, by land or water, arose to handle collecting and distributing systems or lands and credit in their localities, or to interconnect the territory's resources with transport facilities. They gathered people as well as commerce and often preceded much rural settlement around them which, instead, fanned out from these little urban sites. A number of towns (perhaps having had head starts as frontier bases) then gradually grew with hinterland settlement into locally prominent cities. A few, of course, would go on to higher levels of metropolitan significance, to become control points in the region's expanding urban network and so embrace still wider economic realms. Leading places such as these might thus become regionally dominant, while remaining but submetropolises in relation to greater command centres outside their home territory. In any event, they were in and of their particular region, handled the mass of its transactions with other areas, and even when transmitting impulses from bigger outside places of power served as principal directing channels. All this came generally to be the case from St John's to Vancouver, as Canada's five regions built up economic structures organized upon their own metropolitan centres, the prime focuses of their characteristic activities and interests and of their identity besides.

Political structure was also very much involved in the

rise of regional centres, through the legislative, administrative, and judicial systems that integrated regions with their governing cities. Centres that were or became primarily political seats, like Fredericton, Victoria, or Ottawa, exhibited a more one-sided, though certainly real, kind of urban dominance. Essentially economic centres which were not also ruling capitals – such as Calgary or Saint John, Vancouver or Montreal – could still develop considerable sweeps of headship, the last-named most emphatically so. But dominant places that incorporated both political and economic roles had their ascendance reinforced; as was evidenced from St John's, Halifax, and Quebec to Toronto, Winnipeg, and Edmonton. Indeed, the regional capital where legislators and officials foregathered might exert a particular kind of economic weight precisely because of its political functions. For in government chambers there, public policy and funds were assigned to building highways, canals, and other public works in the hinterland and aid was awarded private land, railway, and resource projects – altogether providing government cities with metropolitan capacities that went far beyond exercising a merely administrative sway over regional domains. In short, regions could be constantly influenced, even moulded, by their urban seats of political authority.

Somewhat the same can be said about the social and intellectual authority that emanated from major regional cities. In religious organization, they were abodes of bishops and higher clergy, headquarters for Protestant denominations and their most influential congregations. In cultural fields, universities and professional training and public educational offices came largely to concentrate there, as in due course did libraries, literature, theatre, music, and other arts. It may not be too surprising that élite elements in churches, education, and the arts became so ensconced in major urban communities (government seats or not) alongside the upper ranks of business and professional society. But it should be noted that in these focal places the élite groups joined in attaching a region's social and cultural life to its urban centres of headship, once more fostering the whole area's sense of collective identity. Veritably, in so far as regionalism was a socio-cultural creation – as in part it was – local leading urban groups had much to do with shaping it.

But here we are returning to the realm of opinions and attitudes, where perceptions have their play. In each of Canada's main regions the prominent cities that commanded channels of communication centred flows of information and opinion and thereby acquired an abiding hold upon the area's viewpoints. Their principal newspapers conveyed popular appreciations of events and ideas, interpreting or promoting regional consciousness in the process. Influential urban bodies, from boards of trade to literary associations, regularly pronounced on the area's concerns or aspirations. More broadly, political and economic interest groups – farm organizations, labour unions, co-operative societies – put directing offices in the main regional cities and acquired public forums there. These organizations might have roots and followings deep in hinterland territory, yet the topmost local urban centres offered much more concentrated audiences, more effective facilities as headquarters, and better means of publication – even for farm movements. Hence a region's own metropolitan places came especially to present – even champion – its perceptions and beliefs.

Now these home-area metropolises, or sub-metropolises, doubtless harboured self-seeking interests of their own. No doubt, too, the small-town businessmen or countryside producers beyond their civic limits did not always look to them in love and trust. Still, the rural residents looked to where the action was and aims might be accomplished, to where an urban society with higher prestige provided less restricted scopes and styles or offered much fuller entertainment and excitement. Country dwellers habitually deplored the ostentation, greed, immorality, and crime that weltered in even their own local version of the Big City, but it drew their continual regard all the same. They paid tribute in attention and attitudes – even those of disapproval. Moreover, if prairie farmers, say, denounced Winnipeg's Grain Exchange as the swollen monopoly of the city's wheat traders, or the merchants of minor Nova Scotian ports condemned the domineering magnates of Halifax, hinterland groups in both countryside and city would nevertheless make common regional cause against the perceived far worse evils of dominance from a central Canadian Montreal, Toronto, or Ottawa. In confronting dangers from without, the region's own headship cities indeed became its champions (no matter if self-proclaimed) because these centres could and did strive to uphold their home territories against external dictates and designs. Being on the main path to outside powers, a focal regional city was readily alive to their pressures, and as readily responded. The responses might be calculated and heartfelt together. Their effects were, notwithstanding, to rouse and strengthen the region's sense of communal distinction within its own accepted limits. An 'attitudinal' kind of metropolitan involvement was at work here.

All in all, it does seem manifest that metropolitan-based forces were profoundly instrumental in building patterns of identity in Canada's regions right from the frontiers on. And in doing so, they also ministered to the development of an overall Canadian identity, which is not just some sort of incidental aggregate. The whole is more than the sum of its regional parts. In that context, one should certainly remember that metropolitanism could operate on national levels across Canada as well as inside the major divisions of the country – or again, on a still broader international scale, as well as inside areas smaller still than regions. For keep in mind that metropolitanism signifies a *relationship*, displaying spheres within spheres, not one single entity itself. Here, however, we are getting into conceptual matters that can be better left to the next lecture. We can instead round out this opening survey of the historical workings of metropolis and hinterland in Canada with some reminders of the national context itself.

After all, nationalism no less than regionalism was rooted in Canadian experience, ever since the nation-states of France and England first laid claim to parts of a future Canada. From the early seventeenth century, appropriation, colonization, and war in these overseas hinterlands marked the extension of national empires by two rival metropolitan powers until the cession of New France at the peace of 1763. Thereafter, the anglophone and francophone component groups with a British-held Canada represented two separate heritages of nationalism, a fact acutely plain by the 1820s at least. Obviously more was at work here than regionalism. French-Canadian *nationalistes* came to seek sovereign independence, far beyond regional accommodation. And British-Canadian supremacists upheld One Canada: nationally theirs everywhere. Yet another version of nationality was gradually emerging, a Canadian variety which could reach into both language communities. It appeared in the impetus that spread in the provinces of the mid-nineteenth century for responsible self-government and then for Confederation. It was expressed in the subsequent growth of federal political life after 1867, in national policies of tariff protection and western development, or in the building of the dominion's railway net that linked major hinterlands and cities from coast to coast. Again, these events and projects involved much more than regionalism; and while regional criticisms might be often voiced, so, too, were national sentiments – as federal parties and popular responses could amply demonstrate.

There is no need to depict these features as enduringly set or wholly realized before 1914: just to assert their decided presence by that time. Other than that, I would reaffirm that metropolitan cities entered widely into the development of both national structure and consciousness. Montreal, since fur trade days the heart of a commercial hinterland greater than any region, went on to become the hub of national transport and financial enterprises. Toronto, increasingly reaching beyond its own regional territory, competed with Montreal to west and east, but joined in backing national economic policies that set up checks or offsets to the penetration of Canadian hinterlands by American metropolitan powers. National activities and concerns, moreover, were not only centred in the two leading Canadian metropolises or in the federal capital, Ottawa; they were also manifested in other major cities. A Halifax, a Winnipeg, or a Vancouver assuredly did not live closed in by local ramparts; each was nationally interconnected as well. In fact awareness and perceptions of nationhood were vigorously present in the various leading urban centres for the same kind of reason that regional consciousness was: because they were principal places of concentration for population, information, and opinion as well as chief transmission points between their own regional hinterlands and the Canadian nation-state.

Much more could be added, but it must be left to another occasion. And so I will end today's submission with a promise: that the national as well as the regional impact of the metropolitan relationship in Canada will be given due attention before these lectures conclude. My next, however, will turn to the concepts and analyses that underlie the approach I have adopted. It will consider the systems of ideas that have informed the treatment of metropolis, frontier, or region in Canadian history, under the catchy title of 'Frontierism and Metropolitanism: Concepts Revisited.'

# LECTURE TWO

## Frontierism and Metropolitanism: Concepts Revisited

# Frontierism and Metropolitanism: Concepts Revisited

MY FIRST LECTURE surveyed the relationships of metropolis and hinterland in Canada before 1914 – relations between a dominant urban power centre and its supplying, serviced territory. It dealt with their mutual ties, exhibited both in structures and perceptions, and suggested their significance for aspects of Canadian identity as well. Affirming that Canada essentially arose out of frontiers, I presented the frontier as a furthest and rudest sort of hinterland, notably derived from out-thrusts of the metropolis for new supplying areas of trade and resources. In time, and under continual metropolitan influences, most Canadian frontiers developed into well-occupied and structured regions, that is, into maturing regional hinterlands. I went on to discuss the consequent shaping of Canada's main historical regions, pointing to the operation of metropolitan factors in the process. The final portion of the lecture appraised the role of the metropolis in fostering patterns and attitudes of regional identity, or regionalism, while not dismissing metropolitan associations with national identity. Yet this initial prospectus left a sizeable amount to be made good in my succeeding lectures, of which this one concerns the ideas and inquiries that have gone to produce the interpretation I am offering.

The ideas to be considered, and the concepts they involve, particularly refer to the key terms, 'frontier' and 'metropolis.' Other major terms, such as 'city' and 'hinterland,' can effectually come into an examination of the concept of metropolis, while 'region' and 'regionalism' have already been treated in their Canadian sense during the previous lecture. But frontier and metropolis remain crucial. Moreover, they have engendered bodies of thought and writing: in the one case, an extensive Frontier School of history; in the other, a variety of metropolitan studies in urban sociology, economics, government, and more. The resulting formulations of frontierism and metropolitanism have both held importance well beyond Canada. In assessing them here, we must remain aware of their broader relevance, especially for the United States, the inevitable North American comparison with Canada. Yet our primary focus and continuing concern is with Canadian instances, as we revisit the oft-examined and integrally related themes of frontierism and metropolitanism.

I stress that they ought indeed to be seen as fundamentally related through the metropolitan-hinterland association itself. However different or distant frontier and metropolis might look from one another, they are reciprocally connected, serving each other and developing together (I did not say equally). They stand virtually at either end of a scale in human settlement and activity: the former displaying the smallest, most dispersed population and a limited, simple social or economic life; the latter, the most numerous and concentrated populace, highly specialized and complex in its society of work. Nevertheless, the two ends bracket a single scale and are linked by the measures in between. These are premises, of course. They should become a good deal more apparent after fuller inquiries into frontierism, first, and then metropolitanism, which will elicit my own renderings of both of them.

Frontierism unquestionably owes its chief intellectual origins to the work of Frederick Jackson Turner on the westward flow of settlement in the United States. In 1893 he first depicted the advancing frontier line of settlement – 'the hither edge of free land' – as a dynamic, even a determinant, running through much of American history. The continental development of the United States, its national character and institutions, its democracy and sectionalism, could all be especially ascribed to the creative forces of the frontier in motion and the huge bounties of cheap land it made available. So Turner argued; most definitively in two volumes of collected essays, *The Frontier in American History* (1920) and *The Significance of Sectionalism in American History* (1932). As elaborated, criticized, and revised, his frontier thesis attracted retinues of American historians and, in time, was applied to Canada, Australia, and other lands. It is not necessary for our purposes to detail the contents and adaptations of the thesis, only to acknowledge the vital well-spring of Turner's ideas. Yet several points should still be made respecting them.

First, the idea of the frontier as a moving margin between settled territory and primeval wilderness was a different conception from older European notions of a frontier as a political or military border area, the defensive marches along the forefront of a state. No doubt a frontier in the American or Turnerian sense could have political and military implications: certainly for native peoples faced with invasion it did. It might thus become a zone of warfare with Indian societies and perhaps involve rival white contenders as well. Nevertheless, in the Turnerian version the frontier was basically a socio-economic and socio-cultural marginal zone between 'civilization' and 'savagery' – an area grasped at by transforming settlement, expansively and not defensively, to open up more lands and resources.

Second, his formulation embodied bald assumptions of the moral superiority of civilization over savagery: a belief that American pioneer resolve, initiative, and know-how were near unbeatable in the cause of higher civilizing ends, and that the wilderness indeed lay open, 'free land' for the taking. The presence of native tribes scattered through a vast terrain to which they held ancestral rights appeared at best a passing problem for treaty negotiation to remove, at worst a question to be solved by greater force. Frontierist discourse on 'winning the West,' or on the beneficent march of liberty-loving settlers, was deeply imbued with white ethnocentric presumptions. It gave slight regard to the aboriginal tribes shattered by cultural conflicts or devastated by war and disease, and then moved off to reservations.

Yet third, for all the harsh realities beneath Turnerian ideals of pioneer progress, the sheer weight of civilized power and the numbers behind it did make frontiers advancing margins that appropriated natural wilds. 'Wilds' or 'wilderness' are obviously relative terms, and one can contend that they carry cultural bias. Still, these great North American expanses had on the whole been very thinly occupied by indigenous peoples; and though that occupation had undoubtedly left effects over ages immemorial, the ranging native hunter-gatherers and small village societies of corn growers or fishermen north of Meso-America had simply not done much to cultivate or alter the immensity of natural landscapes. They may have been the happier, living in accord with lasting wilderness. Who can really say? In any case, their homelands were perceived by European newcomers as near-empty, undeveloped wastes; and these the more technologically equipped, more strongly organized invading societies could and would take over. Native inhabitants were seldom sufficiently numerous or well marshalled to check the dispossessing surges for long. In stark effect, Turner's 'free' land became just about that.

Fourth and finally, while Turner or his Frontier School associates largely directed their minds to frontiers of agricultural settlement – as in the vast farmlands of the American mid-continent – they did not thereby disregard fur trade and cattle country frontiers, or those of mining and lumbering, which might draw far less settlement than would the agrarian kind. The vision of free land did comprehend other areas besides arable territories. Frontiers, as a result, were seen as more than moving margins of pioneer farm seekers. More fully, they were expanding supply zones for civilization.

The Turner concept was originally set out well before a recognition of metropolitan-hinterland relationship.

It almost posited the reverse, in fact, by stressing peripheries, instead of cores, as ruling factors in American history. That view at length was challenged in the United States. Turner's portrayal of the frontier West as a renewing source of liberty, democracy, and vitality that virtually infused and animated the established East was met with the query, 'frontier of what?' – and the answer that westward expansion was more truly eastern-derived and really produced new Easts. Be that as it may, leaving the American debate aside, aspects of the Turner thesis can still be applied to Canada's historical development and concerted with a metropolitan approach.

In Canada, as in the United States, the frontier surely represented progressive infringements on the native wilderness and its peoples and carried resource exploitation with it in purpose and result. Nor can one doubt the manifold impacts of the frontier in Canadian history, although it may be shown all the more conclusively to be a dependent, not a determinant, and directed by metropolitan out-thrust, not itself a director. Furthermore, the very sectionalism which Turner regarded as rising from frontier foundations in the United States had a counterpart in regionalism in Canada, even if 'region' has become the preferred word in this country. Altogether, then, by modifying yet utilizing Turner, we can reach a closer conception of the frontier for Canada. It is a marginal area extended into natural wilds by a society engaged in acquiring and developing the soils or other resources of this rudimentary hinterland, through which process the margin gains its own newly emergent community.

Let it be added that Canada's frontiers revealed far less land suitable for farm settlement than did those of

Turner's United States. Apart from the arable western plains (where climate still strongly limited arability), Canadian territories abundantly featured northern forests, rock masses, muskeg, or tundra barrens. And the fertile areas that could support substantial rural populations were much restricted in central Canada, still more so in the Atlantic and Far Western regions. The unrelenting granite of the Precambrian Shield straddled the midst of the country, not the richly fruitful Mississippi Basin, agrarian heartland of the United States. There were no cotton or subtropical plantation kingdoms to develop here, or millions of acres of midwestern cornfields. Agricultural frontiers that loomed so large in Turnerian perspectives were in no way as predominant in the vistas to the north.

In Canada's considerably different context, nonagrarian, commercial resource frontiers stood out the more prominently. They were often capital-intensive and seldom good fields for the pioneers idealized in Turnerian tradition – small, self-employed settlers whose individual enterprise tamed the wilderness with due aid of axe, ox, and sturdy family. Instead, the Canadian kind of frontier was, from the fur trade on, a commercial one, marked by large enterprises and hired contingents of workers. Big, metropolitan-backed business firms arose on the resource frontiers, whether as fur, lumber, or ranching companies, as mine or railway syndicates. They made the outlays in equipment and infrastructure needed to wrest resources from an obdurate land, investments often beyond the capacities of small-scale venturers. Even Atlantic fishing frontiers did not remain a preserve for the little, independent operator: early on an effective division appeared between 'masters' and 'servants,' followed by the truck system that bound fishermen to store merchants' credit. Generally speaking, resource frontiers favoured neither the economic nor social independence of ordinary individuals.

Even Canadian agrarian frontiers showed deviations from a Turner image of frontier democracy based on pioneer individualism. In the Plains West, physical conditions and market problems impelled farm proprietors towards more economically viable large holdings and mass co-operative associations. On eastern farmlands, there were signs of frontier democracy in early backwoods life, yet the curbs of colonial officialdom were never far away. And in Quebec, habitant farmers remained obligated seigneurial tenants right to 1854. Free-ranging individualism could assuredly be seen on Canada's distant reaches, among the fur traders of the North-West, for example. Still, individualism was often curtailed, save among powerful entrepreneurs and urban businessmen pushing unrestrainedly after the resources of new hinterlands.

It is true, of course, that large entrepreneurs, wealthy corporations, and hired (or slave) labour were also much in evidence on resource and some agrarian frontiers in the United States. Self-employed small operators similarly persisted on Canadian margins to varying extents. The point is still, however, the proportionate differences in the cases of the two countries. Canadian historical circumstances, overall, reveal the relatively greater part played by big-interest, commercial frontiers and the narrower role of independent, family-farm pioneering – with comparatively different social consequences to follow. This Canadian condition may itself raise class issues to contemplate, may credibly demonstrate the nexus between frontier and metropolis, or may merely have some bearing on reputed Canadian tendencies to accept orders and stay in line. At all events, the case supports a verdict that the American creed of frontier democracy espoused by Turner had only limited application to this northern country. Here rocks and wilds did not readily give way to the common man, or harsh expanses as happily become self-sustaining, individual homesteads. Writings on Canadian frontier have made that very clear.

2

Among their authors since at least the 1930s, one leading interpreter of Canada's frontiers needs singling out, the eminent sociologist and social historian, S.D. Clark. Delbert Clark's illuminating treatment of frontier themes is best found in four of his volumes: *The Social Development of Canada* (1942), *Church and Sect in Canada* (1948), *Movements of Political Protest in Canada, 1640–1840* (1959), and *The Developing Canadian Community* (1968, revised). But the first-named work set out his main scheme of analysis. In this basic study he identified a series of frontier societies across the country, in chapters that made plain the commercial aspects of Canadian frontiers and their growing urban components. The introductory chapter, which outlined his approach, defined frontier expansion as 'the opening up of new areas or fields to economic exploitation.' The frontier itself was merely the area in which such an expansion occurred. 'Instead of being employed in the Turnerian sense to designate the furthest extended line of settlement,' it referred to 'the development of new forms of economic enterprise,' which produced 'a succession of export staples' from newly opened areas.

This kind of approach can contribute to our own conceptualizing of frontiers. Even if Clark did not represent them as new hinterlands per se, he recognized their economic links back to dominant seats of power, to urban centres and their command groups, and the limits thereby set to local individual initiatives. He also discerned that since 'frontier economic expansion involved the recruitment of capital and labour from outside,' the resulting growth 'made necessary the extension of institutional controls,' exercised variously through monopoly trading companies, the state, the churches, or educational and similar organizing bodies. But because capital supplies were drawn strongly into economic enterprises, other systems or services suffered on emerging frontiers. In fact, Clark noted, lags appeared in their social organization, so that frontiers became widely characterized by degrees of communal disarray and weakened traditional sanctions, by 'social disorganization' disclosed in non-conformity, licence, dissociation, and heady ferments of religious and political radicalism.

His assessments carry substantial weight. They were worked out further in his volume on churches and sects in Canada (the former representing closely organized, traditional denominations, the latter loose-knit Protestant dissentient groups that sprang up on frontiers) and in his study of radical political movements that derived from frontier circumstances. Still, it does appear that Clark overstated his arguments. Frontier religious sects often spread to newer areas from older ones by way of a disciplined and centrally directed missionary effort:

pioneer Methodism with its radiating circuits is a good example. Radicalism was not sui generis to the near wilds, but had origins in outside areas, made links with urban headquarters and newspapers, and often relied on urban followings besides. Clark did not deny interworkings of this sort; rather, he concentrated on just one side of them.

Of more significance, his depiction of social disorganization and dissent on frontiers does not take account of all the evidence. Clearly present there – at the same time – were instruments of authority and accepted social controls which functioned despite any structural lags or shocks of the new. Frontier New France might indeed have known unbridled coureurs de bois. It also felt the ordering restraints of a centralized state, church, and military system – not to forget seigneurialism. In the young Maritime and early Upper Canadian colonies, presumably non-conformist backwoods still lived with local Loyalism and Toryism, garrison posts and gentry authority, as did the opening west with mounted police jurisdiction, capitalist land companies, and railway overlordship. Once more, Clark did not ignore these features, but largely underrated them, though he did himself assert that frontiers duly became accommodated to established order and incorporated within it. In selecting certain attributes as decisive in patterning the frontier in Canada, he provided an interpretation that remains valuable and enlightening, but inconclusive.

Clark nonetheless moved the treatment of the frontier much beyond Turner, by emphasizing its economic basis, the role of major organizing factors acting on it from outside, and (largely through its own rising urban centres) from inside as well. Still further, he viewed frontier expansion as occurring through the successive taking up of resource areas to produce staple exports. Building on these aspects of Clark's work, we can lay out a general historical pattern for Canadian frontier developments in keeping with their regional and urban-metropolitan associations. They can be followed through a series of levels, or phases, in resource exploitation and in the occupation of advancing hinterland margins.

The initial level in this, my, scheme of frontierism is a 'superficial extractive' phase. It was first represented by the migratory Atlantic fishing frontier of the sixteenth century that brought European fishermen each summer to Newfoundland where some set up shore stations to dry their staple harvest of cod. The fur trade, probing inland by the seventeenth century, also fits this phase, involving as it did relatively limited transfers of men and matériel to the frontier area to skim its raw resources for export without doing much to re-shape it. A later example, in the young nineteenth century, was square-timbering which launched new forest staples and frontiers. Still later in that century came the placer mining of the Far West for gold washed down by streams and the open-range ranching of plains and foothills. These enterprises all existed within largely wild natural settings, and while they might give rise to some fixed depots, forts, or camps, they usually produced spotty and often transient occupation. With little question, the frontier hinterlands of this first phase were rudimentary.

There followed a 'committed extractive' phase, well exemplified by sedentary, resident fisheries on the coasts, which led to year-round habitation and port villages in Atlantic fishing hinterlands. Much more clearly, farming frontiers typified the increasing commitment of people, stock, and equipment to the resource margins, whether in the mid-St Lawrence Valley of the 1660s, in the seaboard provinces and early Upper Canada by the 1790s, or in the western regions from the 1870s. This level was expressed as well in the establishment of sawn-lumbering, which brought larger cuts, permanent mill sites, and frame buildings, all affecting both milling centres and rising farm villages. In due course, the committed phase appeared in the west with stock-raising on fenced ranches, and in hard-rock mines sunk deep into western mountains – and thereafter within the northward-spreading Shield. Such kinds of resource-based hinterland activities generally demanded much more engagement of labour and skills, not to mention production goods, workplace construction, and housing. And so frontiers of this second level led to a larger, lasting occupation in steadily altering landscapes. They fostered urban growth, as incipient towns swelled with the mounting flow of staple produce out to market and in time found local markets of their own in the increasingly populated neighbourhoods about them. Frontier areas of this sort could soon no longer be termed rudimentary.

Again in time, a third or 'processing' level eventuated which saw still more intensive treatment of the resources exploited in frontier hinterlands. It was variously illustrated across the country in flour-milling, brewing, or woollen-weaving, by wood-working and carriage- or furniture-making, by meat-packing, fish-canning, or pulp-milling, and in smelting and other means of upgrading basic mine products. Such processing enterprises could considerably augment countryside growth; yet they were often town-centred and in some instances forecast urban factory concentrations. One could claim, in fact, that the processing phase really marked a transition from frontier to maturing region, and to the emergence within it of substantial cities out of towns. Moreover, the latter development was not merely a quantitative change in urban size but a qualitative one also, involving urban functions of a higher order, that is, of greater specialization and range of influence. At any rate, just as frontier hinterlands rose into well-structured regions, so processing concurrently worked within them to augment their population and organization.

But we should recognize – as was briefly noted in the first lecture – that not all Canadian frontier margins became prosperously advancing regional hinterlands. In some circumstances, they might undergo regression and population losses as their primary resource base was dissipated. Even if that wastage did not reach extremes, marketing, technological, or capital problems, fluctuations in yields, and the narrow reliance on one all-important staple resource might still spell setbacks. Downturns or much restricted gains occurred in the Newfoundland fishery, for example, so greatly dependent on its staple cod. And lands of little agricultural value bared by the New Brunswick forest frontier, impoverished farms on thin soils in eastern Quebec, or collapsing towns hit by closed-out mining and forest ventures from Ontario to British Columbia were bleak reminders that frontiers did not necessarily ascend beyond basic resource extraction. Canadian frontier history, like any other, was not foreordained to be consistently a success story.

Regenerative growth also took place, however. That is to say, erstwhile frontiers might replace or at least

diversify their original limited kind of resource exploitation. In some areas once home to simple pioneer
agriculture – especially in southern Ontario – farmers
in the later nineteenth century shifted from staple
grain-raising into dairying, meat-producing, or vegeta-
ble- and fruit-growing for mounting urban markets.
Fishing developed increasing specialties on both
coasts. Lumbering multiplied its products: from pulp-
wood in eastern forests to building supplies furnished
to prairie farms and towns from British Columbia. To
the gold from western mountains, mining added silver,
base metals, and coal, produced iron ore in Newfoundland, coal in Nova Scotia, and silver, gold, and nickel in
northern Ontario. The stress on staple resources
remained in virtually every region, but greater variety
was created too. Beyond that, the growth of factory
industry, primarily but not exclusively in Quebec and
Ontario, brought much larger concentrations of settlement and bigger internal markets. New service activities, burgeoning financial, transport, and electric
power systems, accompanied the sweep of industriali-
zation from late in the nineteenth into the twentieth
century.

Within the now-developed regions of Canada, hydro-
electric plants, factory-made wares, and new amenities
multiplied. Mail-order purchases and farm machinery
proliferated in rural areas; telephones, electric light,
and soon the automobile in the local towns. These were
but a few signs of the regenerative spread of goods and
services now that the barer frontier levels had been
surmounted. Signs like these were apparent in all the
regional hinterlands of Canada by the First World War.
By then, too, their major cities had skyscrapers climb-
ing in downtown business districts, electric streetcars,

crowded inner city housing, and outflung suburbs; all pointing to an abundant urban life in regions that had obviously grown far past their frontier phases. Cities of these dimensions point to the metropolis and metropolitanism – to which we now turn.

3

The term 'metropolis' has conveyed a range of meanings down to its popular, but loose, great-city implications of today. In the ancient Greek world the word denoted a 'mother city' such as Athens, the colonizing parent of new city-states. During early Christian eras, the term came to be assigned to the territorial seat of a presiding bishop, a metropolitan, while in the rising age of nation-states it was applied to the capital city of an entire kingdom. All these designations had lasting import: the metropolis as an engendering parent-place, a seat of institutional authority, and a supreme political headquarters. But the broadly applied word still lacked much conceptual content, above all with respect to economic meaning. That was not to be compellingly provided until the seminal work of Norman S.B. Gras published in 1922, *An Introduction to Economic History*. In this book he gave the metropolis, the outstanding urban centre, far more explicit definition through his conception of economic metropolitanism.

Gras, the Canadian-born founder of business history at Harvard, discerned that the rise of a pre-eminent city or metropolis did not involve just the growth of a particular urban place in itself, but also the development of an area around and beyond it, in which it functioned as a controlling central point. Accordingly, he described 'a metropolitan economy ... of producers and consumers mutually dependent for goods and services, wherein their wants are supplied by a system of exchange concentrated in a large city which is the focus of local trade and the centre through which normal economic relations with the outside are maintained.' What Gras had essentially recognized was the metropolitan-hinterland relationship; but there was more. He also projected a succession of stages through which a city rose to be a metropolis by achieving dominance over a large trade-and-service hinterland, the other component of a metropolitan economy. First, the aspiring urban place built up commercial ascendancy, through providing warehouse, market, and distributing facilities for the hinterland territory. Second, manufacturing was developed and interwoven with the area, whether in the city or its surroundings. Third, city-led improvements in transport organized the whole economic system more closely and efficiently around its centre. And, fourth, that centre amassed financial power in banking, insurance, and investment firms, which underwrote its trade dealings, outward or inward, as well as mobilizing capital for the whole area's development and managing its access to credit. Financial dominance thus crowned the city's status as a mature metropolis heading its own economic domain.

Gras's formulation of metropolitanism in the 1920s came at a time in the United States when the ecological approach of the Chicago School of sociologists was influential and much in harmony with his own depiction of an interacting, interdependent economic community. The school's exponents broadly dealt with social systems within an organic or even biological frame of reference, noted symbiotic relationships in their functioning, and conceived the activities of dominance largely as co-ordinating and organizing rather than coercive or exploitative. Without doubt Gras took a similar view of the crucial matter of dominance in his metropolitanism, regarding it not pejoratively, but as a constructive, ordering capacity that shaped and advantaged the whole metropolitan-hinterland community. Some later inquirers were to adopt a very different view of metropolitanism, treating it as a dominance-dependency relationship that darkly represented the bondage of abused subjected areas to plundering metropolises. Gras and his ecological contemporaries, however, mainly looked to the bright side.

In my own view, it makes more historical sense to see dominance neither as naturally benign, producing the best of possible worlds, nor as innately baneful, by prejudgment. On the one side, in spite of the mutuality and inter-reliance so basic in a metropolitan system, frequent discords may appear among its different group interests. Drawing a simple biological analogy of the metropolis as 'head' and the hinterland as 'body' really conjures up a pretty sick-looking organism, with its head engaged in frequent rows with various other parts of its anatomy. On the other side, to display metropolitan workings as essentially oppressive and parasitical, pushing dominated areas deeper and deeper into backwardness, is no more historically convincing. There is altogether too much counter-evidence. It thus looks sensible to consider chief-city dominance as a widely evident historical fact that can have either positive or negative consequences according to circumstances. That, at least, does not subscribe to now outmoded ecological presumptions – or prohibit adapting Gras to further use. In any case, his concept of a city-based system did fit in with the mounting interests of sociologists, geographers, and others in urban studies which made the metropolis a significant concern of urban specialists in both America and Europe by the 1950s and 1960s. Yet our own prime concern remains with Canada and pertinent developments there.

In this country, the metropolitan concept as pioneered by Gras did not have much impact at first, though the McGill sociologist, C.A. Dawson, who wrote in the 1930s on Canadian western frontiers of settlement, did have students inquire into it. Still, it seemed much more applicable to densely populated, intensively developed communities in Europe or the United States than to the near-frontier and staple-crop experience of Canada. Hence that master economic historian, Harold Innis, virtually set metropolitanism aside; to his mind Canadian cities grew in a different pattern mainly framed by staple production. Nevertheless, in a brief article of 1933 Innis did discuss 'the rise and decline of Toronto,' to reach conclusions, he said, 'largely based on the work of Professor Gras.' Much more significant, Innis's own classic writings on Canadian staple industries or long-range transport systems powerfully testified to the constant interplay between power cores and resource peripheries – and to 'the discrepancy between the centre and the margin' that was embodied in such a heartland-hinterland relationship. In all this work there were strong underpinnings for the subsequent study of metropolitanism, just as there would be in Innis's later work on the history of communications. He laid broad foundations for examining metropolitan development in Canada, no matter if he did so without that deliberate purpose.

Others proceeded purposefully, in particular Arthur Lower. Initially, he had been prominent among Canadian historians in applying Turner's frontier thesis. He indeed asserted in 1930 that 'American democracy had a forest birth' and regarded the frontier in Canada as generating an egalitarian society whose 'frontier spirit' typically contended against 'vested interest.' Such a contest of indigenous freedom and imported privilege ran through Lower's noted general history of Canada, *Colony to Nation* (1946). Well before then, however – from the later thirties – he had also taken up the idea of metropolitanism, which he put forward explicitly in *Colony to Nation* as well: thereby expressing the reality that 'metropolis' and 'frontier' were not necessarily divorced or contradictory concepts, but could notably redound on one another. From his studies of forest frontiers and lumber trades, Lower had come to perceive the pulls of metropolitan power on Canada's resource hinterlands. In fact he described the nub of the metropolitan relationship as 'demand centres calling on supply areas.' This was still a somewhat one-sided designation that did not cover the other fundamental aspect of the two-way flow, demand areas calling on supply centres. But Lower chiefly espoused the pejorative view of metropolitanism as inherently subjugating and exploitative, sucking a territory dry because 'business had to go on.' He thus conceived it as an unavoidable accompaniment of technological civilization and the concentration of power in great urban centres – yet at debilitating costs to the hinterlands. That bleak assessment was graphically presented in his much later work of 1973 on the square-timber trade of the eastern British American colonies, aptly entitled *Great Britain's Woodyard*.

In a way, then, Lower kept to his early frontierist leanings, maintaining the view from the periphery of the hinterland dwellers against city plutocrats or metropolitan high-rollers. His younger near-contemporary, Donald Creighton, took an opposite perspective: from the key urban centre where business interests sought to dominate the territories beyond. To Creighton, these were dynamic interests that created a grand design of trade and transport around which a transcontinental Canada would itself arise. Certainly in his work their powers of dominance appeared far from negative; they were concerned with far-sighted building, not profit-draining, whether the protagonists represented Montreal fur merchants and forwarders, CPR entrepreneurs, or nationally minded, business-oriented politicians like John A. Macdonald.

Creighton conveyed this positive viewpoint in his brilliant *Commercial Empire of the St Lawrence* (1937), which portrayed the forceful merchants of Montreal as architects of a great commercial state erected along the river trunkline and its connections inward, the precursor of modern Canada. Though the empire he traced from the 1760s to the 1840s broke down, the vision of a St Lawrence-centred unity behind it persisted to be realized at a later time. This Creighton also described in writings on Confederation and the young Canadian nation-state, most dramatically exemplified in his two-volume biography of Macdonald (1952 and 1955). But his single-volume history of Canada, *Dominion of the North* (1944), had already put forward the essential theme: from the French period on into the twentieth century, the country took form about an east-west, St Lawrence based trade and transport system, in which the business elements of major urban places like Montreal, Quebec, and Toronto played weighty parts.

Creighton's Laurentian approach was of course

partly anticipated in the economic histories of his close friend, Harold Innis. The latter's *Fur Trade in Canada* (1930) had earlier linked the country's emergence to its waterways and the St Lawrence in particular and seen the very staking out of Canada's territorial bounds as an outcome of the great business enterprise in furs. Creighton's Laurentianism, however, extended beyond economic developments, resources, markets, and technology to aspects of political, cultural, and class interests; that is, to still more general Canadian history, mainly recounted in strong centralist-nationalist terms. But did this amount to metropolitanism itself? Not in my opinion. Like Innis, Creighton contributed much to an understanding of metropolitanism in Canada, without specifically adopting it; and that is not to criticize him but solely to state a point. If, for example, he dealt with business personages or groups in Montreal rather than with the city itself, he met his own historical purposes admirably. Nevertheless, while his Laurentianism came near to metropolitanism, they were not one and the same. The latter had further range and concern, not to mention concept. Creighton saw the reach of central business power over hinterlands and the influence of metropolitan traffic systems. But only quite late in his career, and largely in passing, did he expressly refer to metropolitanism, after the authoritative body of his own work had long been set out.

W.L. Morton looked beyond Laurentianism while marking the constructive value of the metropolitan-hinterland idea. In a trenchant article of 1946, this western historian, Manitoba-born and bred, criticized the Laurentian approach as too largely taking a central Canadian imperial view and neglecting the history of the western hinterlands except as tributary areas for costly nation-building schemes. At the same time, Morton recognized that the west's development had proceeded within the metropolitan structures extended from the east, whether they pertained to markets, transport, and finance or to religious, intellectual, and political organization. A good deal more explicitly than Laurentian writings had done, he pointed out the workings of metropolitanism. But though he saw its positive as well as negative attributes, he also upheld the cause of regional history – as a necessary offset and counterpoise to centralist bias, whether Laurentian or metropolitan in kind.

Morton produced outstanding works in regional history: *The Progressive Party in Canada* (1950), a penetrating account of western farm protest, and *Manitoba, A History* (1957), a benchmark in the study of distinctive regional societies in Canada. Yet while he knew and applied metropolitan-hinterland ideas, Morton came, by the 1970s, to present regionalism and metropolitanism as almost in antithesis, the first, naturally, expressing 'regionality,' the second 'centrality': a fundamental dualism in Canada's development. This view implies that a metropolis only acts on a region from outside (and so merely imposes an extraneous, centralist dominance); it overlooks the possibility that a metropolis might also grow up within a region, intrinsic to it – rather like Winnipeg in Manitoba. Morton, then, took up metropolitanism in more positive ways than Lower had, more expressly than Creighton did, but, notwithstanding, left metropolis and hinterland in a state of dichotomy instead of integral relationship.

It was D.C. Masters who in 1947 most forthrightly and consistently applied the concept of economic metropolitanism originated by Gras. He did so in *The Rise of*

*Toronto, 1850–1890*, which he introduced as 'a study of the rise of Toronto to metropolitan status,' a term connoting 'the dominance of an urban centre over an adjacent area or hinterland.' Masters directly employed Gras's four basic economic factors in metropolitan growth – commerce, industry, transport, and finance – but he also observed (and showed) that the scope of a metropolis 'involved much more than mere economic dominance,' since it exercised political, cultural, and social influences over its hinterland as well. He asserted further that the 'rise to metropolitan status has powerful repercussions on the metropolis itself,' on the size and extent of its urban settlement, on its physical appearance, on its social fabric, and on its living conditions. All these features were demonstrated in Toronto's case, to produce an instructive Grasian model.

The consequence was that by the 1950s, when I myself took up metropolitanism in Canada, there were lots of thought-provoking materials at hand. They led me to a first article in 1954, 'Frontierism and Metropolitanism in Canadian History'; and in ensuing years I continued my endeavours in articles, chapters in collective volumes, and a more recent single volume, *Toronto to 1918* (1984). The detailed list is best left to footnotes, along with works of able Canadian contemporaries who have materially contributed to my own metropolitan approach. That approach, derived from Gras's original ideas and influenced by the others discussed, still needed shaping to meet further issues. Dealing with them will occupy the final portion of this lecture.

4

An outstanding issue to be dealt with – referring back to Gras – is that his conceived progression of stages by which an urban centre rose to become a metropolis does not sufficiently accord with actual Canadian experience. Gras's four basic economic factors in metropolitan growth certainly tended to come into play here in major phases over time, but not in the set sequence of commercial, industrial, transport, and financial stages that he had described. Instead they often appeared in overlapping phases or even in a different order. Moreover, a Canadian city which did attain a leading position might function as a dominant commercial metropolis and transportation hub while lacking a strong industrial component or while possessing financial institutions that were mostly just branch agencies of firms located elsewhere. Such a city could be large and prominent in its own territory, yet still would not rate high according to Gras's envisaged sequence. It seems, in fact, that his pattern was most applicable to the old-established, closely settled societies of western Europe, his own principal field of study, than to the circumstances of a primary-resource, thinly populated country like Canada – and that, in this respect, Innis had been right.

Furthermore, under Canadian conditions, provisions for transportation usually much preceded significant industrial undertakings. Here transport systems generally grew in near conjunction with commercial activities, for without the means of moving traffic over the distances and obstacles of an undeveloped continent, scant commerce and few urban centres of commerce would have sprung up at all. Canoe routes and Indian trails had sufficed a frontier fur trade. But these primitive traffic systems were inadequate for close settlement which instead went hand in hand with transport advances – in coastal shipping, lake and river steamboats, St Lawrence canals, and, above all, railways.

Major transport services, which tapped or filled hinterlands and fed urban places, were all but primary in
Canadian metropolitan growth that had virtually to
start from scratch. Moreover, transportation readily
related to the needs of communication, to moving information and opinion as well as goods and people over
wide distances. Communication facilities like press
and publishing, postal, telegraph and telephone systems, each urban-centred, shared in metropolitan
development. And most of them were firmly established well before factory industry at last grew powerful
in Canada during the late nineteenth century. As for
financial growth – which did strongly mark the final
level reached by top Canadian cities before 1914 – this
had shown much earlier manifestations. Commanding
banks had appeared in Montreal, Halifax, and Toronto
between 1817 and 1832, and loan and mortgage houses
proliferated there around the mid-century. All in all,
Gras's prescribed succession of stages for metropolitan
organization was breached repeatedly in Canada.

If, however, Gras's four basic economic factors are
treated instead as characteristic metropolitan activities
or functions, whether or not they operated in a set
sequence, then they fit Canadian experience with little
difficulty. One or other might become especially evident at various times, but all were inherent in the rise of
metropolitanism across Canada. At first they were
evinced in the commercial, transport, and financial
undertakings which external metropolises extended
into this country. Later they were displayed by growing
internal metropolises, beginning with commercial and
transport activities to which industrial and financial
ones were added. Hence these major economic functions may all be dealt with as attributes of metropolitan

dominance over hinterlands, whether in Canadian frontier or region. In operation, they produced focusing and controlling structures and influenced broad perceptions of interest in both metropolis and hinterland. Without forgetting the political and other non-economic factors in the metropolitan process, one still can hold that the most basic and prevailing ones were economic – in keeping with Gras's master concept, thus amended.

The term 'metropolis' can accordingly be given a more satisfactory definition for present use. It denotes a dominant large city, whose commanding status essentially expresses the commercial, transport, industrial, and financial functions of control or influence which it exerts over extensive and productive hinterland territories. These four economic attributes exist in varied degrees and combinations in the metropolis, and work in concert with political, social, and attitudinal factors that contribute to the city's role of headship, but the economic aspects of the metropolis are most fundamental. That, at least, is the position I have reached.

Yet more has still to be said on non-economic issues. For instance, to the political attributes of the metropolis (remarked in the first lecture) military factors might be appended. Decisions to garrison a strong point or set up a controlling naval base could bear on metropolitan growth from Halifax and Quebec to Victoria. Such military developments generally occurred during the earlier phases of metropolitan activity in Canada to 1914, although their results could be enduring. Much more apparent in succeeding periods were social factors, most notably the part played by urban élites through which the dominance of leading cities was particularly exercised. I also mentioned in my previous lecture the religious and cultural establishments that were located in major Canadian centres and which shared with their business and professional counterparts in tying hinterland populations to metropolitan hegemony. Now it needs adding that the social controls and influences centred in the top elements of a metropolis might be transmitted either directly to the hinterland or through the lesser élites of subordinate cities within that domain. Of course, these satellite élites, tied in as they were, might not serve merely as repeater stations: they could reveal their own critical tendencies and local feelings. Upper ranks in Sherbrooke did not necessarily echo Montreal or Trois-Rivières, Quebec. But in the main they duly conveyed the precepts and attitudes sent forward from the central communities.

Moreover, metropolitan social influences did not only operate on upper-class levels. Among Canadian workers, unionism gradually spread links through the hinterlands, yet focused headship in dominant places where large industries arose. Similarly among the working classes, benevolent and ethno-religious societies like the Orange Order came to cluster in leading cities, with affiliate units throughout the countryside. As for the middle classes, they stretched multiplying social networks out from metropolis to hinterland – interlacing sets of business partners, agents, dealers, and clients. Economic in purpose these ties plainly were, but they largely relied on social relationships of mutual confidence. In addition, widespread middle-class interests in religious missions or in moral reform causes like temperance came particularly to be based in the principal Canadian cities, from where zealous impulses went out like waves to the hinterland. Metropolitan social dominance thus came to comprehend powerful uplift movements led by worthy city bourgeois, through central initiatives and organizations that did not spring from rural revivalism.

The social aspects of metropolitanism thus cover far more than the activities of top-drawer élites. Yet the conduct of power through élite networks remains a significant theme to trace in metropolitan relations because these groups are so involved with dominance and decision-making, obvious features of power élites. Of late years, the general idea of social networking has attracted academic attention – and no wonder, when it can be as readily applied to class or gender groupings as to businesses ranging from small firms to multinational companies. An important critique of the 'metropolitan thesis' by Professor Donald Davis of Ottawa has held, in fact, that networks of élites expressing social distributions of power deserve first priority in urban historical study in Canada instead of the spatial-distribution approach taken by metropolitanism. He has asserted that élites not cities have wielded dominance and have done so through core-group loyalties and ties of 'kinship, amity and clientage' that transcend place. He argues that cities themselves had neither aims of control nor power functions. Those rather belonged to individuals or elements within an élite who would increasingly exert them without much concern for their own particular urban location.

The issue thus raised has positive value; certainly, in bringing out the importance for metropolitanism of networks other than spatial networks – whether they are social networks or networks of technology, information or faith, for that matter, all of which can equally enter into metropolitanism. But the critique goes too far in stressing the social context simply by itself and in underplaying no less basic facts of space and place. The truth remains that social formations such as urban élites exist within spatial settings even today and may decidedly identify with places, from local town to regional city or prestigious metropolis. Members of social groups not only relate to ties of kinship, amity, and clientage, to ethnic, class, or corporate loyalties, but to where they live and work, raise families in neighbourhoods, and share a perceived community and its attitudes. They define themselves in locational, urban, or regional terms, not just in the light of class awareness or roles in some space-transcending corporate body. These truths actually are self-evident, yet now seem to need recalling. A sense of place is real and potent, beyond any issue.

Despite claims that we live in a global village, the huge improvements in communications have not obliterated spatial distinctions. In many ways, they have made societies more aware of them. And when it is claimed that transiency increasingly erodes ties to place – or, as particularly concerns urban élites, that the shifting of managers around far-flung company posts replaces old-fashioned allegiance to a specific city with that to a modern unlocalized corporation – then several answers rise to mind. First, that even should this now be so, an élite's commitment to developing its own city of residence was in plain sight throughout long urban ages. Second, that transiency at any level is nothing new in urban life, least of all in a country of immigration like Canada, and was visible throughout its past. Third, that a city in any case held swelling numbers of long-term residents, including

élite members who inherited or soon adopted the
urban society around them as their home community.
And fourth, that the newer notion of loyalty to organization as a surrogate for home turf begins to look a little
dubious in itself, given recent sweeps of take-overs,
'down-sizing,' and other blows that must shake loyal
devotion to the Big Outfit. In brief, spatial dimensions
cannot just be set aside. They belong at the heart of
social networks which in reality do operate across
space and between metropolis and hinterland – not in
some abstract continuum.

There is still the other part of the issue raised by
Donald Davis: 'Ambitions, like dominance and power,
are attributes of elites not cities. Nor do cities exercise
economic control; entrepreneurs and business corporations do.' One may grant that specific living persons,
not urban heaps of numbers or inanimate brick, wood,
and metal, assert ambitions and economic control. One
could also grant that élites do not actually exercise
power or dominance; their human components do. But
this kind of word-game is sterile. The fact is that élites,
cities, or metropolises are all human collectives and are
normally treated as such: as having aims, functions,
and significance beyond the lives or doings of their
particular members. The same, after all, may be said of
some other collective entities like nation, state, or government, class or corporation. Each will constantly
have ambitions or power designs attributed to it, past
any ascribed to specific individuals or groups within
the collectivity. The great city cannot be excluded from
similar treatment. Beyond that, while a metropolis may
fairly be regarded as a vehicle for the power of élites,
they no less serve as its own power instruments. Again
neither half of the equation can be set aside. And while

it follows that historic metropolitan dominance would be largely exerted through élite elements, it does not follow that non-élitist lower-class or middle-class residents failed to share ambitions and loyal attitudes regarding their home city or, indeed, felt no benefits from its economic and other forms of dominance.

Once these points are recognized and allowed for, however, inquiries into social networks can be validly comprised within the metropolitan approach to broaden the examination of metropolis-hinterland linkages on the various levels of Canadian society. In the upper ranks, for example, one could trace the lines of allegiance spun between central core élites and satellite communities by judicious marriages or preferments to official posts, through interlocking directorates, through military comradeships in earlier historical periods, and later through the right school or college affiliations. Radiating ties of kinship may be found spread over space on every level, whether in leading city mercantile houses or prime financial circles; among the uncles, nephews, and brothers-in-law who joined in lesser chains of store-keeping; and amid the farm and worker families whose lines rank back to kinfolk in older lands – kinfolk who might thus be drawn to settle near them.

Kinship, besides, might well be put as clanship to cover the social bonds sustained across distance by Scots and some other migrants, or the bonds of birthplace as well as blood which provided affinities between settlers from the same home neighbourhood or town. Certainly ethnicity was a powerful force in many social networks extending from core areas to peripheries. Along with shared religion, shared ethnic origin had its place in the webs that interwove metropolitan élites and in the links that ran through other classes of society in city or hinterland region. In addition, ties of amity were exhibited in political dealings that allocated patronage and public services around the hinterland, ties of clientage in economic transactions that distributed contracts, purchases, and investments from the centre. But in any event, social networks of affinity and attitude pervaded many of the activities of the metropolitanism I have described.

In the third lecture I will try to connect these deliberations on metropolitanism and frontierism and my earlier outline of metropolitan-hinterland relations with the concerns of identity in Canada – national, regional, or otherwise.

# LECTURE THREE

## The Metropolis and Identity in Canadian Experience

# The Metropolis and Identity in Canadian Experience

I N CLOSING the previous lecture, I said that my next would seek to relate metropolitanism and frontierism with the concerns of identity in Canada; that is, to link the workings of the metropolitan-hinterland system with the rise of Canadian regional and national identities in particular, though not excluding ethnic or other kinds of identity. The prime agent to be followed through this inquiry into collective Canadian experience before 1914 will, of course, be the metropolis, for, as our discussions have shown, the weight of impelling forces and decisions lay strongly with the metropolitan place. The frontier, however significant, was still an outlying, thinly developed, and highly dependent adjunct of the metropolis, and even the far more developed regional hinterland largely remained subject and directed. All the same, frontier and region must naturally enter into the examination of metropolitan connections with Canadian identities as hinterland components of the key metropolis-hinterland relationship.

One could too easily spend an entire lecture defining identity and its psychological bearings, noting that Canada might aspire to world records for the longest-running identity crisis or going over the reams that have been written on national and regional identities in Canadian history, literature, and social science. I venture to raise the matter yet again solely because of the implications of metropolitanism but do not propose further extensive inquiries into definitions. Instead, I would simply associate identity with community – and once more with structure and perception, as I started out in these lectures. The collective identity of a community arises both from its structure (variously comprising social, cultural, economic, or political elements) and the perceptions of its own distinctive existence. The community becomes identified as such by those outside it and self-identified by those within. In other words, it develops a communal identity, whether of town, city, region, or nation. Thanks to the abundant pluralism of Canadian society, moreover, there are quite plainly hosts of other communal identities. Many of them might look very limited in scope, if we should pick upon a single ethnic group, a religious body, or a workers' organization in a local town; but these same groups can represent considerably less limited identities on a regional or national scale. In fact, what we are contemplating are different levels of collective identity, from the most confined and limited to the nation-wide – or, perhaps better, a series of identity-spheres within spheres, in which the smaller ones have the more homogenous contents.

Still, all the major forms of identity in Canada's past decidedly remained limited: that of class by religion and ethnicity, at least, and the two latter in the same reciprocal way. We might conceivably add further identities of gender, family, and generation as yet not largely traced through Canadian historical experience and again find them mutually limiting. Regionalism and nationalism have also set bounds on one another or been affected by the other spheres within them. One might ask whether the nation-state would not at any rate constitute a final, sovereign sphere: a silly question in Canada! Aside from the restraints of colonialism and British imperial supremacy (continuing well past 1914), Anglo-Canadian nationalism has been limited by that of French Canada and vice versa, central-state authority by provincial; while the expanding presence of the United States has brought forth a kind of supra-national or super-continental American sphere that circumscribes the Canada national one. Thus Canada is a land of limited identities par excellence, although that need not be inevitably a bad thing.

In any event, regional and national identity, our main concerns, have inherent spatial limits as well, which are obviously expressed in terms of territory and location. And though such other major collectivities as class, creed, or ethnicity might not seem by nature to be as spatially defined, they also take on distinct meaning and character from location – where they are placed. A mass of workers in a resource industry, for example, becomes signified and characterized as the Ottawa Valley lumber proletariat, a group of religious settlements as the Mennonite community of Manitoba. In short, we once more encounter the sense of place, an ever present definer of identity, whatever various social critiques may say. That powerful sense conveys human configurations of space: whether in the physical disposition of sites of concentrated population and areas of diffused occupation or in the mental images that differentiate the 'in-here' urban community from the 'out-there' rural one. In either case, continued interactions across actual or envisioned space are copiously displayed in the exchanges between town and country, between city and region, between metropolis and hinterland. Their interplay builds historical experience which pervasively influences all sorts of communal identities, above all those of region and nation, essentially related as they are to spatial patterns. And given its powers of dominance and leadership, the influence wielded by the metropolis necessarily stands out.

I am not attempting to claim that metropolitanism alone or in itself shapes identity – a gross extravagance – but rather that it makes a weighty contribution which thus far has gone almost unrecognized. In Canada's case, as I have noted, a good deal of thought and paper has already been expended on analysing its nationalism and regionalism and a fair amount on Canadian class, ethnic, or religious communalisms, much of it very useful. But I do want to make a plea for more, if not equal, time for metropolitan inputs and involvements. We are properly ready by now to regard women's history, family history, working-class history, historical demography, and more as embodying great societal factors which demand study. The same pertains to the great societal factors that underlie metropolitan-urban history. One might recall that its root relationship, that between the town and the country, runs through ages in the world's experience of city-led civilizations. It also bears recalling that the root word behind 'civilization' is, in truth, *civis*: the citizen, not subject, who inhabited the city-state, the *civitas*.

So much for grandeur; now to work. I will proceed by first looking at metropolitanism and regional experiences of identity in Canada to 1914, beyond the generalizations offered in my opening lecture. Then follows national identity, stressing that regionalism and nationalism are no more dichotomous or necessarily opposed than are metropolis and hinterland: reciprocity and mutual reinforcement can apply to each as well as contention and confrontation. The salient but still more limited identities of class and ethnicity will be touched upon in passing; to conclude with some thought on where all this may leave the question of a Canadian collective self in a bilingual, multicultural North American country inhabiting a polyethnic world.

2

Let us start with identity in the Atlantic region. The fact that no metropolitan city within that territory established significant ascendancy across the whole area expressed the 'subdivided' nature of Atlantic regionalism, marked as it was by entrenched provincial loyalties and local sentiments. In the absence of any one regional metropolis able to organize and focus the entire Atlantic hinterlands, three chief places parcelled them out instead. St John's headed commercial and political life in Newfoundland, still a separate dominion for some four decades past 1914. Halifax, the Nova Scotian capital and citadel, could seem more eminent in the region as a leading centre of ocean trade, shipping, and defence. But it shared headship even in the Canadian Maritime provinces with New Brunswick's Saint John, which

grew with lumber exports and shipbuilding, and sur-
passed Halifax in size during the latter half of the nineteenth century. In addition, the small cities of Fredericton and Charlottetown possessed the authority of
provincial capitals. All in all, the three most prominent
Atlantic cities apportioned but did not master their
region as a unit.

One might think that this urban pattern just represented more general partitioning factors in the Atlantic
region: its geography of islands and open coasts
beyond any close unified control; its resource base,
mainly in fish and lumber, which did not promote large
population centres; and the four historic provincial
entities that pre-empted the terrain. Thus it may well
be that the manifested Atlantic metropolitan structure
was the effect of bigger regional causes, but I do not
claim that top cities are prime causes in themselves.
What is of consequence is how they did relate to matters of identity. And it is not enough to say that each
leading place in the Atlantic area simply reflected its
provincial confines. The picture was more complicated.
True, St John's' dominion to 1914 was largely that of
Newfoundland, yet its hold was spotty even over fishing
outports as near as those on Conception Bay and considerably affected by enduring close connections with
business houses in metropolitan Britain. Halifax, tied in
with London, Boston, and the West Indies, long faced
rivalry from lesser ports in its home province, while its
own trading territory extended beyond to New Brunswick's North Shore and Prince Edward Island. And Saint
John, linked to Liverpool and Portland, commanded
much of New Brunswick, especially the lumber hinterlands that rose to the interior Appalachian ridges; yet it
reached as well into the Bay of Fundy shores of Nova

Scotia – and, after the railway was built in the 1850s, to Shediac on the North Shore and into Prince Edward Island.

In sum, overlapping metropolitan domains in the Atlantic area were both less and more than provincial, as was the region's own collective identity. Because this was apportioned, some have contended that it did not exist, that there were only the separate provincial entities. Yet quite aside from their shared elements of geography, economy, social life – and even political behaviour – I would argue for a distinctive composite Atlantic identity. Certainly, it came to be perceived as such from Canada beyond it and was evinced from within by common responses to 'outside' Canadian power. These responses, which remain today, were clearly displayed in the Maritime Rights movement after 1918 and still earlier in the region's discontents with Confederation in the 1880s. More important here, this explicit regionalism was deeply involved with the metropolitan experience.

Because it was less strongly based, Atlantic metropolitanism was the more exposed to the power of outside centres, stemming from metropolitan places in Britain or the United States and from central Canadian cities by the 1870s (the mid-nineties in the case of Newfoundland). The Atlantic regional cities stayed very much subject to external markets and often reliant on outside funding for development, looking to British metropolitan trade laws in one era, Canadian federal policies in another. Moreover, the Atlantic hinterlands were never far from the sea and its lines of dependency outward: the fishing frontiers largely faced east to the ocean; the forest frontiers were not set in western continental wilderness but lay adjacent to the seaboard. And though the peoples of the Atlantic community might be marked by a tough pride in themselves, the stamp of lasting battles with hardships and constraints, they also revealed in both city and country their particular experience of subordination to outside dominance. This did not begin with Canadian Confederation. It dated far back to the rigorous treatment of seventeenth-century Newfoundland by the ruling London metropolis as merely a huge English fishing ship moored overseas, or to the harsh fate of eighteenth-century Acadia as a pawn in the world-wide contest of French and British metropolitan forces.

Nevertheless, over the years, a group image of resilient, pragmatic resistance to external power became embodied in the Atlantic identity, to be especially nurtured in the headship cities of the area as the centres of its regional élites, cultural institutions, and social networks. This did not mean presenting unqualified opposition. Pursuing accommodation was the more realistic way, whether by seeking 'better terms' for political federation or in adapting to a national economic system, as Halifax and Saint John did through gaining recognition and development before 1914 as Canadian winter ports. By and large, the Atlantic metropolises were increasingly integrated into Canadian metropolitanism, while continuing to sustain Atlantic interests, causes, and opinions – just as regionalism and nationalism grew integrated in Canada, yet remained themselves.

Turning to the Quebec region, the historical experience of identity among its francophone inhabitants is beyond all doubt. Yet does it represent regionalism or nationalism? For our purposes, the matter may be judged as one of difference in degree, not kind. Granted that national intents usually fasten on political realizations, which in the form of sovereignty reach a great deal further than do regional designs. Even so, nationalism still constitutes but one more level of collective identity, persuasive or coercive as it can be. Or, put in other terms, a national community represents a sphere beyond the regional society; the two need not stand in contradistinction or mutual exclusion. So it appears with a Quebec identity. It may incorporate Québécois aspirations to separate nationhood; and it certainly has, from the Papineau radicals of the 1830s to the Péquiste sovereignty seekers of our own day, with clerical, literary, and academic *nationalistes* in between. At the same time, however, from Papineau to Parizeau, there has always been the other major element in Quebec's identity that has sought a secure francophone community within a larger Canadian entity. Quebec regionalism, then, can express both components; they are not categorically exclusive; indeed their members shift back and forth. At least, it has broadly comprised both groups till now, and surely did so to 1914. But, further, Quebec regionalism also had to encompass the substantial anglophone minority in a French province, a minority which was disproportionately powerful because of its entrenchment in the urban business élites, especially in Montreal, long a prime metropolis for both Quebec and Canada.

As metropolitan cities, Montreal and Quebec, the provincial capital, left deep imprints on the total Quebec experience over more than three centuries. The fact was that the Quebec region, from its early growth within New France, was decidedly urban-centred. The Marie-Chapdelaine syndrome, conveying a rural world of sturdy habitants with sturdy families in sturdy farmhouses, has never had more than partial relevance. New France began with a commercial base, Quebec, which rose with the fur trade as port and seat of authority well before a settled farm frontier spread along the St Lawrence. Moreover, the uniting river route that bore the vital fur cargoes was controlled by its two key towns: Quebec commanding the access from the exterior, Montreal the entry to expanding commercial hinterlands in the interior. While the growth of farming in the St Lawrence Valley unquestionably served town markets and developments, it remained a minor subsidiary to the long-range, urban-directed commerce in pelts. And as a people, the inhabitants of New France were moulded not simply by local agrarian life on the seigneuries but by the metropolitan fur enterprise that led on through the Great Lakes to the Mississippi and the Saskatchewan. Montreal and Quebec, holding dominant roles at the heart of the great trading advances inland, left an equally great heritage in experience to the French-Canadian community.

The British conquest of the 1760s, of course, transferred external metropolitan supremacy over the St Lawrence domain from Paris to London, brought on the rise of an English-speaking commercial class, and displaced French merchants from the control of major urban business activities. Of necessity the French-Canadian mentality became more rural than it had been, or perhaps more inclined to the consolations of religion and agrarian virtue. Yet the Quebec region continued to be urban-focused, organized on Montreal and Quebec, which were now growing into cities and becoming still more dominant regionally, even if chiefly directed by British mercantile interests. Moreover, the city of Quebec took on a new and influential importance for French Canadians following the introduction of representative government to their province in 1791. Henceforth an elected assembly at the capital could express the views of the French-speaking majority – a provincial offset to British economic mastery – and with the movement forward to fully responsible rule, the province of Quebec at Confederation was left politically in the keeping of its French community. Accordingly, the provincial capital gained a unique position as the seat of the sole Canadian regime controlled by French Canadians, ready to defend their communal security or assert their collective aspirations. The image, and fact, of this ancestral city as both political champion and cultural guardian became basic to French regional identity before 1914 and has scarcely lapsed since.

Within the region in economic terms, Quebec City largely dominated the less well favoured eastern portions of its province, Montreal the more thriving western districts. There was a traditional rivalry between them, but the much greater business power of Montreal made itself felt across the whole provincial realm, not to mention huge areas outside. As a fur metropolis, Montreal had virtually extended its hinterlands to the Pacific before the passing of the St Lawrence fur trade in 1821. It then became a main emporium for the rising inland settlements along the Great Lakes, forwarding them goods up-river, bringing down their products for export overseas. By Confederation, Montreal enterprise had added to wholesaling and shipping large engagements in canals, railways, banking, and rising industry. After Confederation, the city's trade and traffic spread beyond Ontario across the opening west, and eastward through the Maritimes; its banks extended from the Klondike to St John's. In the booming early twentieth century, Montreal not only ranked supreme in Canada as a commercial, financial, and transport metropolis, but rose to be North America's largest grain port as well.

For all that, Montreal's impact on Quebec regional identity was qualified by its very associations far beyond Quebec territory and by its own internal French-English division. Though the city of Quebec retained something of the same split, its English elements (quite prominent through the nineteenth century) did not match those in Montreal whose anglophone populace was relatively much larger and more powerful. Despite the economic grasp of the English Montreal élite, however, it had increasingly to meet the provincial authority of francophone politicians, while French residents faced the dominance of large-scale English interests both over Montreal and the nearby countryside. To ignore the adjustments which these groups reached for effective coexistence, to see only cross-purposes and alienation, would be to misread the record of experience. Nevertheless, the profound social division in Montreal, the main metropolis, could not but affect Quebec regionalism in general. On the one side, it underwrote and empowered the province's anglophone minority as nothing else could have done. On the other, it tended strongly to heighten the French Canadians' awareness of their vulnerability and so to urge more *nationaliste* responses. It was no accident that the Lower Canadian rebellion of 1837 took place mostly in Montreal's environs. The weight of influences centred in Canada's prime city perforce exerted telling impacts on Quebec regionalism. And the defensive-assertive francophone identity which marked it so preponderantly, truly owed a large amount to the workings of metropolitanism.

The Ontario region showed no such keen cultural divide before 1914 or long afterward. Besides, its decisively leading city, Toronto, combined both economic and political headship, along with a widening hold on Ontario opinion and regard. Regard, may I remind you, need not signify approval, only a felt need to watch and note – so that, for a 'Hogtown,' it was the attention which counted. And there is no doubt that Toronto drew notice, by building its ascendancy in the fertile Canadian lakelands up the St Lawrence right from its start in the 1790s as garrison base and capital of the farm-frontier province of Upper Canada. Filling with British immigrants and denominated a city in 1834, this growing Lake Ontario port soon outdid rivals such as Kingston and Hamilton. Railway construction in the 1850s made it a regional rail hub, while after Confederation, in what was now the well-developed province of Ontario, the city added financial and industrial strength to the commercial and transport dominance it had already acquired over Ontario hinterlands. Toronto, in fact, took over much of the region from Montreal's earlier hegemony and in the young twentieth century was challenging that sway in other regions – particularly the western plains – as well as pushing out new mining and lumbering frontiers for itself in northern Ontario. Without question, by 1914 the Lakes metropolis was second only to Montreal in Canada overall and was both a competitor and a complement to the bigger St Lawrence city in many areas outside Ontario.

There is a question, however, not of Toronto's ascendancy, but of what Ontario regional identity it found to influence. It has almost become a cliché in some quarters to assert that Ontario did not develop a significant

regionalism, because it so blithely identified itself with
Canada in general, and because this potent, wealthy
province was not led to any sheltering regional consciousness when the whole country seemed its oyster.
That is the contention, or the indictment, at times put
most forcefully in other Canadian regions. But it deals
in assumptions more than experience. I would submit
instead that a perceived and self-aware identity
emerged in Ontario long before 1914 and that Toronto
metropolitanism had more than a little to do with it.
Besides, even the rich and confident can have character
– approve it or not.

Nineteenth-century Quebec undoubtedly ascribed a
distinctive if not admirable character to Ontario,
regarding it as sharply etched with Anglo-Saxon Protestant bigotry, particularly in Toronto. To be sure, Toronto
and Ontario might return similar compliments about
Quebec Catholic intolerance. The fact remains that
through many decades the identifying marks of firm
religious and 'racial' convictions were evident in
Toronto and Ontario together, whether during the separate schools controversies of the 1850s and 1860s and
the two Riel risings or on imperial issues around the
end of the century. Patently, too, the views of the major
press, the political leadership, and Orange populism
centred in Toronto were echoed across the regional
society. To note that Ontario to 1914 could be effectively
designated Protestant, British, and Orange Tory by no
means tells the complete story – it leaves out its sizeable Catholic minority, its increasing non-British frac-
tions by the First World War, and the Grit Liberalism
that ruled its provincial government from 1871 to 1905.
Nonetheless, the Protestant, British, and conservative
traits ran deep, even in the Grits themselves. Asserting

that Ontario did not display regional identity in these respects is a somewhat unconvincing claim. In the same way, it would be hard to deny the leading part so visibly taken by 'Tory Toronto' in standing for British ties and Protestant rightcousness within the regional community.

Other than this, regionalism was surely revealed to large effect in the Clear Grit liberal movement that swept pre-Confederation Upper Canada, aligning urban Toronto leadership with the Upper Canadian farm hinterland in joint defence of the region against Lower Canadian and Montreal power. This successful alliance directed by the prominent Toronto Liberal and businessman, George Brown, and backed by his *Globe*, Upper Canada's leading newspaper, at one and the same time expressed the regional outlook of Upper Canada/Ontario and the impact of Toronto metropolitanism. That combination kept Gritism strong in the Ontario community well into the twentieth century.

Still further, the long campaign for 'provincial rights' waged against federal authority by the Liberal regime at Toronto earnestly espoused regional sentiments. And during the vexed disputes over Ontario's western boundaries, there were not only spirited appeals to identity (as in the campaign ditty, 'The Traitor's hand is at the throat, Ontario, Ontario'), but also, when the battle seemed won in 1884, the *Globe's* delighted crow: 'Ontario as now definitely bounded possesses within herself all the necessaries and potentialities of a great nation.' Overdoing it, perhaps; but it was no less the response of Toronto metropolitan enterprise, looking to open new western and northern hinterlands within its own provincial grasp. Moreover, there was regionalism here that was far from inconsequential, strongly derived as it was from specific Ontario experience. It was embodied, too, in more than the chief provincial metropolis, Toronto, being implanted as well in Ottawa, Hamilton, London, and a medley of robust, middle-sized cities in this, the most urbanized, affluent, and aggressively expansive of Canada's regional entities before 1914.

In the Plains West and Far West the experience from which regional identity springs was naturally shorter. On the prairie the day of the wheat frontier had scarcely ended by 1914, while in the mountains, settlement had only started with the first gold frontier of the late 1850s. Nevertheless, by the opening of the twentieth century, both western regions had produced major metropolitan cities in Winnipeg and Vancouver, and other western urban centres were also enlarging substantially. The fact was that frontier development and urbanization had gone on here in near partnership. During the sixty years or so since the wilderness fur trade had begun to retreat from its western holdings, metropolitanism had become a direct and vigorous presence within the settled west.

On the plains, Winnipeg had grown since the early 1870s from a trading hamlet outside the walls of Upper Fort Garry to the most populous and commanding city of the Canadian prairies. It was their transport gate and railway hub, their biggest wholesale distributing point, and their essential wheat market for sales outside by way of Winnipeg's dominating Grain Exchange. Rising farm organizations might seek to break the hold of the big merchants on the exchange. But in other dealings, Winnipeg's commercial élite could gain more regional support; for instance, its successful endeavours into the 1890s to get the control of the grading of western wheat transferred to Winnipeg from Toronto and Montreal, the western rail-rate differential it extracted from the CPR in 1886, or its repeated challenges to that eastern company's monopoly of through traffic, shown by concerted appeals to the federal government and by seeking other mainline railways, ultimately built.

The burgeoning Manitoba metropolis largely led the way before 1914 in promoting causes of the Plains West. Still younger western cities, however, shared in fostering the views and interests of the regional society: Regina and Edmonton, become capitals of the new provinces of Saskatchewan and Alberta in 1905 – rail and distribution centres also – and Calgary, emerging from the ranching frontier to focus farmlands in southern Alberta, tap coal-mining districts, and even start into the oil and gas of Turner Valley by 1914. Furthermore, as well as structuring plains hinterlands about themselves, the principal centres radiated strong images or opinions to their surroundings. They did so through Winnipeg's authoritative *Free Press*, Edmonton's potent *Bulletin*, Calgary's irreverent *Eye Opener*, and numerous other media agents of prairie regional metropolitanism. And on the exposed plains – exposed both to nature and to outside controls – these internal metropolitan agencies did much to identify and fortify the region's sense of community, to produce what was conceivably the most lustily declared regionalism in Canada.

Strung out along Pacific margins or between high mountain walls, the Far West produced still another version of regionalism, focused on two principal centres: the island capital of Victoria, which rose into a city in the 1860s thanks to its hold over the Fraser and Cariboo gold fields; and the mainshore lumber clearing, Vancouver, which mushroomed after the arrival of the CPR in 1886 into a transcontinental terminus, an ocean and coastal port, and henceforth a chief point of access to the resources of the mountain hinterlands. By 1900 the emerging metropolis of Vancouver was decisively replacing Victoria in economic headship. As provincial seat of government, however, the older city still exercised wide influence on the British Columbian community, and it had already taken a lead on regional stands, notably in the 1870s, when snail's-pace progress on the projected transcontinental rail line invited angry reactions in an underpopulated, underdeveloped, and bleakly disillusioned British Columbia. Victoria, once capital of a separate colony, centred demands to break from federal union with the distant, unheeding, and all-but-unknown Canada. Separation was staved off by new promises from Ottawa and subsequently answered by the completion of the CPR. Yet this was graphic evidence of an incipient Far West identity focused on Victoria which did not really disappear.

Even though a booming Vancouver had so largely sprung from national and eastern commitments to the continental rail line, it rapidly took on the role of a regional west coast metropolis at the head of its own area's economic hopes and interests. In fact, the city's eager boosting spirit and lively concern with development enterprise well characterized a British Columbian identity, seemingly the most mercurial in Canada: at one moment reflecting sharply on its unheeded isolation and dependency, but at the next switching to visions of bonanza blessings and potentialities as high as the surrounding mountains. That again was the product of Far West regional experience, mediated through aspiring Vancouver metropolitanism. An illustration I like comes from pre-1914 Vancouver, where enterprising junior boosters, Chamber of Commerce types, would march through the city, chanting fervently to a drum beat: 'In 1910, Vancouver then, will have a hundred thousand men.' And it did, if women be included – a chauvinistic note on which to end our dealings with regionalism!

## 3

Regional identity has require more space than will national identity, largely because of the need to show that metropolitan forces could fully express 'regionality' (W.L. Morton's word) no less than they could 'centrality'; that is, could refer to the pivotal national unit. In essence, few would deny the centralizing powers of metropolitanism, and so would not deny their part in national growth above or beyond the regional domains. It is still necessary, of course, to relate metropolitan factors to the actual development of national identity in Canada overall. And that may again be done in terms of major metropolitan places setting their marks on Canadian communal experience – here in the sphere of the nation-state itself.

One might open the national theme by looking far back in experience, to the extension of French and British empires over Canadian territory, a process commonly labelled imperialism, but one which also denoted the export of nationalism by two chief metropolitan power centres, Paris and London. In that respect, the fall of Quebec to Wolfe's forces produced a decisive victory for the British metropolis and nation-state. Moreover, strategic success in the overseas hinterland owed a great deal to two highly metropolitan instruments: the regular forces of Britain brought out and maintained by seapower. And after the Conquest, in a British-held Canada, the two divergent 'nations' of French and English later discerned by Durham still had been planted there through either the bygone dominance of Paris or the continuing sway of London.

An emerging Canadian nationalism instead – one which was not just a transferred colonial version of British allegiance and which could comprise French Canadians prepared to enter partnership for the joint home-rule of Canada – assuredly was gradual in its own evolution. Still, it came: by way of movements in the several provinces for self-government, inevitably centred in their chief cities, then through the drive for federal union (also urban-led) that achieved a Canadian transcontinental state by 1871. There were, as well, pressures arising from the expansive forces of American metropolitanism which had so often to be met. The resulting, yet accompanying, sense of national identity no doubt had many roots, but the rise of a Canadian national entity out of a colonial existence notably represented the progressive replacement of British metropolitan dominance by the advancing metropolitanism of leading Canadian cities.

Rising Canadian metropolitanism on a national scale was powerfully evident in Montreal by the Confederation years and increasingly in Toronto thereafter. But the national capital, Ottawa – sourly described by Goldwin Smith as 'a sub-Arctic lumber village converted ... into a political cockpit' – built up its own kind of metropolitan dominance, nationwide, as federal politics, institutions, and government service grew in scope. National policies of tariff protection, railway building, rate subsidies, and western development affected a great deal more than any particular regional interest or authority. The programmes and projects of Ottawa-based metropolitanism could and did invite critical, even hostile, reactions in some regions. Yet national sentiments beyond regionalism were also engaged, as federal elections would show. Altogether, by 1914, on the even of the brutal testing of the First World War, a continental Canada that transcended all its regions had a substantive national structure and a widespread perception of national identity – all markedly influenced by Canadian-grown metropolitanism, whether centred in Montreal, Toronto, Ottawa, or in other cities that might seem more regionally confined.

Indeed, it should be reaffirmed that regional metropolises across Canada were not at all cut off from national linkages, but were attached to them, echoing the point that metropolitan systems embodied complementation as well as confrontation. From Halifax to Vancouver, the regionally dominant city became integrated into national metropolitan networks: as a major branch headquarters for Canada-wide chartered banks and financial houses, as a national port or rail nexus, or as a main satellite centre for communications and industrial operations which were tied in beyond the region. In consequence, just as a regional metropolis maintained its share of national interests and activity, so it might also share significantly in national attitudes and identity. To repeat, there did not need to be any sharp antithesis between the realms of regionalism and nationalism. A metropolitan place could relate to more than the one sphere, and the regional did lie within the national. Furthermore, Montreal and Toronto themselves clearly possessed regional as well as national dimensions, while Ottawa was both national capital and a subregional metropolis with its own rich lumber hinterland. In similar fashion, a Saint John, a Quebec, a Winnipeg, or an Edmonton lived in national as well as regional relationships.

And speaking generally, Canadian metropolitan cities maintained constant influence upon developing national identity through their dominant holds on both structures and regard. Pronouncements made on national matters in these centres of power and decision carried strong weight, whether issuing there from party, business, professional, or labour leaderships. What thus was said or done reflected the access of these cities to trunk lines of information across the country and their ability to instil a position taken through their own communications nets. Because of their prominent place in the fields of learning, arts, and education, moreover, the main metropolitan communities could both elicit and confirm national images or interpretations, and very possibly do so in fuller, more lasting ways than could other elements within the country. In literature, painting, or school indoctrination before 1914, the themes put forth might invoke the values of Canada's rural life or the wonders of its landscape, but the work was centred in the metropolis: just as the 'national' paintings of the Group of Seven stemmed from Toronto-located artists surveying that city's Precambrian hinterland.

To examine in any detail such aspects of Canadian identity as were fostered and transmitted by the metropolitan centres would take a lot more time than my few remaining minutes. Instead, I can only glance at some notable and noted attributes of Canadian nationalism – beginning with one so basic that it may sometimes be passed over: the consciousness of, and commitment to, a recognized national entity. Canada's leading cities definitely held large stakes in national interests, whatever their regional stakes. Again, these dual sorts of concerns could be either complementary or confronting, but coexisted in any case. The upshot was a very Canadian condition, shown both in headship city and supporting hinterland, in which views of national identity were limited by regional perceptions, and regional by national in turn. Here, too, there is a distinctive Canadian coexistence of identities wherein the balances can shift over time but the conjunction has endured. And that condition has been very much associated with the Canadian experience of metropolitanism, which displays a relatively few large cities (truly large, proportionately) that organize great segments of territory into both national and regional estates, then tend to serve as power-brokers between them – but thereby accentuate limits on identity.

Other attributes frequently claimed for Canadian identity include its mosaic or multicultural pattern, its small-'c' conservative proclivities, and its disposition to 'peace, order and good government' under duly constituted authority. No one could substantiate these claims in several sentences, much less spell out their full affinities with metropolitanism. But taking them as granted, this much might be said on each in succession. Multiculturalism, even by 1914, found root in the growing immigrant groups in most large Canadian cities, and these newcomers (neither French- nor English-speakers) spread out on metropolitan networks to northern resource frontiers or into western hinterlands. Yet, long before, the groundwork for a pluralized state and society was laid in the special guarantees of French-Canadian and bicultural existence provided by the

Quebec Act and in Ontario separate school laws that were basically initiated to safeguard the religion of a large Irish Catholic minority. Developments from such crucial legal precedents as these effectually cancelled the prospects of a publicly established monoculture – quite a different historical experience from that of the United States. Multiculturalism, and the varied ethnic identities which it endorses, has not simply been the product of recent Canadian decades. Yet, virtually throughout, it has been the main metropolitan cities which have formed the principal testing zones, the front lines in cultural clashes that subsequently led to pluralist answers. Not rural French Canada as much as Montreal, not Orange Ontario towns as much as Toronto – and not Manitoba villages as much as Winnipeg's North End – were crucibles for the multicultural components which flowed into a Canadian amalgam, thus ensuring that ethnicity remained another major limiting factor in national identity.

As for the generalized conservatism so often said to typify Canada, its leading cities have been seen about as often as the habitats of ruling conservative-minded élites, representing the particular power in Canada of big metropolitan business closely aligned with political authority – ever since the monopoly days of the Hudson's Bay Company. While these upper level groups could be economically venturesome at times, socially and politically they were tied to established doctrines and patterns of behaviour in which, down to 1914, the middle and lower classes of the same major cities very largely shared. This may raise a question of class identity. How far had such a thing emerged in Canadian cities before that date? There is ample nineteenth-century evidence of various kinds of class responses on issues of unionism, housing, social services, and a good deal more, but less evidence of explicit, guiding class-consciousness. Though that might sometimes be discernible, whether among tycoons, hard-driving manufacturers, or labour activists, it was more generally true that class identity was substantially limited, not only by national or regional allegiances, but still more by locality, ethnicity, and religion, all of which could cut sharply through class lines. In a broad sense, therefore, conservatism did remain characteristic across the class levels in Canadian cities, for all the political liberals they might hold or the undoubted rise of labour and socialist radicalism within them in the last decade or so before 1914. And this predominantly conservative outlook was strongly projected by the cities.

In social terms, in the stress on public order, public morality, and respectable but responsible authority, Canadian metropolises made a somewhat different contribution to the national entity about them than did those of the United States. It almost seems that the latter had never quite got over the American frontier, or at least that its myths of an heroic age of lawlessness continued to live within them. Canadian cities, however, knew a different tradition, where frontiers had essentially stayed under metropolitan control and lawful authority – unless briefly on the North Saskatchewan in 1885. Be that as it may, Canada's chief cities have seldom indeed come up to their American counterparts in municipal licence or civic disorder. Montreal under the austere magnates of St James and Sherbrooke Streets was no Babylon on the St Lawrence. There is scarce need to cite the persistent image of Toronto the Good, city of churches. And even in seaport Halifax, merchant and garrison overlords kept a firm lid on wharfside excesses. To be sure, Vancouver's west-coast effervescence might stand out among its western Canadian peers, but looked far more staid and sober when compared to its American urban neighbours down the coast. Still further, I would argue that the Canadian metropolises did not just reflect orderly national predilections or dutiful social codes, but, through their wide powers of influence, imparted and sustained such attributes of national identity to be perceived from Halifax to Victoria.

4

So much for national features. These final minutes can be used for some words of conclusion, summing up, and afterthought. In these lectures I have considered metropolitanism, its reciprocals, frontierism and regionalism, and its frequent accompaniment, nationalism, in terms of Canadian experience throughout. It is worth re-emphasizing, however, that the metropolitan-hinterland relationship can be found all around the world and that its global embrace may show many international aspects or, in more recent times, the spreading activities of multinational corporations. Fortunately, a national framework can nevertheless serve adequately to 1914 as long as it is kept in mind that, well before then, metropolitanism also operated through colonial empires. In that regard, is the modern multinational, in its high dealings with states and potentates, perhaps the old English East India Company writ large? No – I think not: the East India Company probably showed more responsibility.

At any rate, the Canadian case that I have presented obviously has connections beyond our national bound-

aries and instructive analogies with metropolitan-hinterland developments in the United States at the very
least. Similarly, helpful comparisons (and contrasts)
can be drawn between Canadian and Australian metropolitan experiences, each involving a few big cities in
huge expanses, sited marginally around an inhospita-
ble central land mass, cold and rugged in the one case,
hot and arid in the other. In fact, Australia in significant
ways remains more usefully comparable to Canada
than the densely populated American superpower; for
the latter with its much larger and more numerous
cities and a multiplicity of smaller urban places exhib-
its considerably more intricate and less direct workings
of metropolitan forces. But I will let that be, and again
revert to my Canada First mode of treatment.

In pursuing such a Canadian mode, I have admit-
tedly been engaging still in national history, such as
Donald Creighton did so effectively and wholeheart-
edly in his writings, and such as William McNeill, my
predecessor as Creighton Lecturer, did not do in his
valuable and stimulating discourses here in Toronto
two years ago. In fact, Professor McNeill then rather
implied that national history was passé in view of the
impressive outline of world history he set forth. My own
clinging to a Canadian approach is neither to support
Creighton nor to deny McNeill, both of whose reputa-
tions would scarcely be affected by an intervention
from me, one way or the other. But while accepting
McNeill's convincing exposition of a polyethnic world
in which the homogenous nation-state was largely a
West European and transitory creation, thriving chiefly
between 1750 and 1920, I still find plenty of room for
national historical examples profound in cause and
effect: including that of Canada considered in its metro-

politan, urban, and regional context. (And, anyway, I creep in under McNeill's wire, which he strung at 1920).

Finally, I would say that there are nationalisms and nationalisms, whether in Sweden or Sri Lanka, or as displayed by the high-powered, state-of-the-art American model and the low-powered, sometimes creaky Canadian product. I do not mean to be either Pollyanna or Cassandra in avowing that, having looked at metropolis and frontier, region and identity in Canada's past history, it does seem to me that the malleable national and regional entities which have developed here from that experience – perhaps ambivalent, sometimes at cross-purposes, and persistently limited – are in no way ill adapted for an eroding, fragmenting world where strong national doctrine and indefensible patriotic stands may not be the future's way at all.

... What follows in the fourth and last lecture is really a return to Canada's metropolitan beginnings. And yet it should show how deeply threads of nationalism, regionalism, and identity were interwoven there as well.

# LECTURE FOUR

## External Metropolitanism in Canada's Opening Age

# External
# Metropolitanism in
# Canada's Opening Age

T HE RISE of an internal
metropolitan system within Canada grows very evident
across the nineteenth century, made plain by the dominant cities developing in its regions from east to west.
Yet the play of external metropolitanism upon the
country is visible much earlier. As each region was
successively opened to Europe, outside metropolitan
communities came greatly to affect Canadian experience and the emergence of future centres in Canada.
Well before 1800, in fact, and through a long opening
age, the external metropolis was strongly interacting
with Canadian hinterlands, whether they then were
still wilderness frontier or had become half-fledged
colonial holdings. This founding age effectively began
about 1500, after John Cabot's voyage had spread word
of the fishing wealth available in waters off Newfound-

land. Hence we, too, begin here with the Atlantic region, the initial overseas frontier of Europe.

As fishermen voyaged each spring to Newfoundland, or dried their catch at summer fishing stations on the island coasts, there was not much sign of metropolitan direction and organization behind their multiplying private ventures. Yet when in 1583 Sir Humphrey Gilbert proclaimed English title at St John's's deep sheltered harbour – before thirty-six fishing ships from France, Spain, Portugal, and England – it was a sign that the international, undirected, and nearly unorganized phase of the Newfoundland fishery was already passing. Metropolitan interests were becoming increasingly involved. England's defeat of the Spanish Armada in 1588 heralded an era of decline in the seapower of Spain (which had annexed Portugal) and in the Spanish and Portuguese fishing fleets besides. During the same era, the concentration of English fishing stations on the eastern side of Avalon Peninsula led to an emerging English Shore along this closest reach of Newfoundland to Europe, which also held the chief shipping rendezvous of St John's, while the French fishery stayed more scattered, spreading out the coasts to westward. Furthermore, England began exporting quantities of Newfoundland 'dry fish' to Iberian and Mediterranean lands: for this cod, lightly salted and hard dried, made a low-bulk, long-keeping protein food even for tropical markets. And it was soon to supply West Indies plantations as well.

Still further, a lucrative staple trade in dry cod, which returned subtropical goods or Spanish gold and sack (white wines), fostered entrepreneurs in England. From the start, the fishing ships which annually visited Newfoundland from west of England ports had been provisioned by local merchants in these ports who then marketed the catch at home. But as the long-distance export commerce grew, so did the West Country towns and their merchants, battening on the Newfoundland fishery from Bristol around to Plymouth and Poole. No one truly dominant centre developed for this vigorous leading group, in time identified as the Western Adventurers, but it could fairly be termed a collective metropolitan interest concerned with dominating a resource hinterland. Plymouth and Poole became prominent shipbuilders for its lines of transport. Bristol, second-largest city in Tudor England, had sent out Cabot in a Bristol ship; and at Dartmouth (neighbour to Plymouth), the Newman firm by 1604 was embarked on some three centuries of dealing with Newfoundland – where Newman's Port is still sold in the 1980s.

Nor was this all. The national metropolis, London, sent 'sack ships' to Newfoundland to buy cod direct for the Spanish trade. And entrepreneurial minds in both London and Bristol projected a colony on the island, which would provide a resident base and allow a longer fishing season to increase the cod supplies for export. This, of course, was part of a surge in colonization ventures evident in western Europe during the young seventeenth century: joint out-thrusts from metropolitan cores by state power and business enterprise together, in which the central political regimes chartered companies or groups of proprietors to settle and develop new domains abroad, while these chartered bodies counted on the trade monopolies or rights to land, resources, and governance that thus were granted to them. So came Port Royal in Acadia by 1605, Jamestown, Virginia, in 1607, Quebec in 1608; and in 1610 a little colony beside Conception Bay on the north side of the Avalon Peninsula in Newfoundland, planted there by the London and Bristol Company.

That company soon gave up its efforts in the hard island setting, though some company settlers and later arrivals stayed on as shore fishermen. They had, however, to face sharp antagonism from the visiting overseas fishermen (and the merchant Western Adventurers behind them) who both resented competition from residents and feared their encroachments on the fishing stations which the visitors took up each summer. Nevertheless, pockets of settlement did form along Conception Bay and in the vicinity of St John's, while in 1638 a new enterprise backed by London sack-ship owners began a larger colony at Ferryland well south of St John's. Under the firm governorship of Sir David Kirke the colonists rose to some 500 by mid-century, carrying on a small-boat fishery at various harbours in the eastern Avalon, if much outnumbered each summer when the overseas fishermen arrived. Yet the latter's hostility only grew with mounting settlement and was keenly supported by the Western Adventurers' powerful lobby in the English parliament. Governor Kirke was a royalist, under a royal charter. When the Civil War in England brought the overthrow of crown by parliament, Kirke was removed in 1651 by the victorious parliamentary Commonwealth. Metropolitan events remote from the hinterland had ordained the fate of the Newfoundland frontier. It was left virtually ungoverned as well as colonized no more: left to the sway of the visiting fishery and its West Country leadership.

That this crude dominance was endure for over a century reflected not only the parliamentary weight of the West Countrymen but also the prevalence of mercantilist ideas in England. Mercantilism (which had close ties itself with metropolitanism) aimed at national wealth and self-sufficiency through external trade, by expanding exports while largely confining imports to goods that could not be produced at home and by fostering the nation's seafaring for commerce abroad. The Newfoundland overseas fishery seemed to meet these purposes admirably. It supplied a far-reaching export trade, one which returned exotic products from warmer climes and plantation colonies. Moreover, the crews who yearly crossed the Atlantic to the fishing grounds were seen as a reservoir of trained seamen, available to merchant fleet or navy in time of national emergency. Claims such as these for the visiting fishery were repeatedly, and no doubt sincerely, voiced by the West Country dominant group, especially the 'nursery of seamen' argument. More significantly, these views were accepted and acted upon by successive central regimes in England; nor did the restoration of the crown in 1660 make much difference.

Instead, mercantilism became entrenched more fully at the Restoration, as did the hold of the overseas fishery on Newfoundland. New regulations of 1661 enforced the local authority of 'fishing admirals,' a rank given by custom to the master of the first ship to reach a fishing harbour for the summer season. The rough justice dispensed by these admirals (by 1676 embracing any crime committed in Newfoundland) was scant indeed for any settled inhabitants. In truth, fishermen freely harassed them, at times looting and destroying houses in attempts to drive the settlers out. Their entire removal was more than once considered by home government officials, though never quite carried into effect. And as if this was not enough to demoralize abused, unwanted, hinterland residents, with no rights to land or law of their own, they were also drenched with cheap liquor brought by New England ships. The opening of trade with a rising New England gave Newfoundland another outlet for its dry cod and a nearer source for many supplies, but the plentiful West Indies rum supplied as well by Massachusetts captains spread 'tippling houses' and violence all the more widely. Brawls, ruffianism, endangered families, or helpless misery were the marks of this harsh kind of pioneer individualism. Frontiers are said in many cases to evince breakdown or institutional disorder, licence, and lawlessness. These were surely displayed in seventeenth-century Newfoundland. Yet behind all its keenly apparent anarchy lay decided metropolitan policy and control.

Settlement nevertheless continued, unintended, for the locally based fishing it lived by offered real advantages over the visiting or migratory enterprise. A sedentary fishery unquestionably provided a longer season, as well as other catches besides cod, in time including seals. Moreover, while the visiting fishery demanded sizeable investments in ocean-going vessels, idled over the summer, the resident fishermen needed only small boats, for sack ships or the ubiquitous New England carriers took their cod away to market. To meet the resident competition, in fact, or to share in its advantages, some of the migratory fishermen even took to wintering over for a year or so at a time, and some of this temporary population remained. Thus, despite violent abuse and official disregard, the number of year-round inhabitants of Newfoundland – who mostly came themselves from England's West Country – slowly increased to over 1200 by late in the century, amid a total summertime population of around 9000. It bears noting, too, that the Newfoundland Act of 1699, which served mainly to consolidate the supremacy of the visiting fishery by statute, did also grant a limited right of private property to island residents. And this act also gave them an appeal from the judgments of fishing admirals to the commanders of warships in the defensive force which each year convoyed the seasonal fishing fleet to and from Newfoundland.

By this time, matters of defence and war were emphatically affecting metropolitan policy. From 1689 to 1713, with only a few years' break, France and England fought in Europe and America. In Newfoundland the French had established a fortified base and colony at Placentia, farther west along the south coast, moved by mercantilist and naval concerns for their own transatlantic fishery. During warfare about the island Placentia was raided, but French forces ravaged the eastern Avalon, the English Shore. Moreover, St John's, now fortified, was taken by the French in 1708 and held to ransom. Yet British successes elsewhere outweighed such hinterland calamities. Hence at the peace signed in Europe in 1713 France gave up Placentia and recognized Britain's title to Newfoundland, though it received an exclusive right to catch and dry fish on the empty western coastline – a French Shore not to be yielded till 1904. Until then, indeed, external metropolitan prescriptions held mastery over the furthest margins of the island.

In its settled portions, metropolitan designs extended from England similarly continued to dominate long after the peace of 1713. Fixed in mercantilist perceptions, the London authorities went on upholding the migratory fishing interest and striving to check still-growing settlement in Newfoundland. West Country ships, however, were often the very instruments of this growth. They carried out extra hands and even passengers to cut costs: men who might be left to winter in the island and prepare for earlier fishing starts in spring or merely abandoned in the fall to seek other work; women brought as servants who then stayed on to raise families of their own. These immigrants confounded metropolitan policy. Yet external metropolitanism has often promoted effects in distant hinterlands that were neither purposed nor desired at the centre – see the American Revolution. At any rate, in Newfoundland the year-round inhabitants reached 7300 by mid-eighteenth century, while their share in the total summer population advanced to 30 per cent in the 1730s, to 50 per cent in the 1770s, and by century's end to nearly 90 per cent. Much of this settlement came from Ireland, where the outbound fishing ships put in for final supplies and cheap workers. Again, metropolitan-based transport served to move new elements to the hinterland, depositing the Irish arrivals largely in the eastern Avalon, especially in or near the chief landing place, St John's, while the longer-implanted English settlers tended to push the fishing frontier on westward to new outports along both the northern and southern coasts.

Accordingly, as the eighteenth century wore on, the frontier stage began to pass in Newfoundland, at least in its original Avalon setting. An organized regional hinterland was taking form there, however rude or incomplete. In social institutions, Anglican missions and schools appeared between 1726 and 1744, the first Methodist society in 1765, while in 1784 a Roman Catholic prefect apostolic was appointed. The metropolitan authorities even took gradual, dilatory steps to erect a political structure, not thereby abandoning their own mercantilist perceptions, but only in order to handle practical problems of public order in this increasingly populous hinterland community. From 1729 a royal governor was re-established for Newfoundland, usually the naval commander of the annual fishing convoy. In summer he was present in St John's, which became his capital; in winter the few justices of the peace appointed for districts on the old-settled English Shore were feeble substitutes. Still, they pointed the way: on to a criminal court, set up by the naval governor in 1750, and ultimately to a supreme court for the island created at St John's in 1792, which ended at last the long and dubious sway of fishing admirals.

The West Country interests fought hard against the crucial act establishing a supreme court, but by then the migratory fishermen were but a dwindling fraction compared to a permanent population in the island of about 15,000. Neither immigration alone nor the economic worth of the resident fishery was wholly responsible for the decline of West Country influence. Great conflicts reaching far beyond the fishing hinterland sharply affected the migratory enterprise: the Seven Years' War that saw the cession of New France by 1763 and the American War of Independence extending from 1775 to 1783. To the overseas fishermen these widespread struggles brought wartime dangers on their transatlantic passage, soaring insurance and labour costs, and the loss of seamen pressed into the Royal Navy. Determined efforts to reverse the consequent decline in the visiting fishery were made by metropolitan officialdom after the Seven Years' War, but they were negated in any event by the coming of the War of Independence. A decade later, the French Revolutionary and Napoleonic Wars that began in 1793 and lasted to 1815 spelled the final disappearance of a once-supreme fishing hegemony over Newfoundland.

External metropolitan dominance did not disappear, however. It altered in form. Over the eighteenth century, as West Country vessels had taken to carrying and supplying as well as fishing, so West Country merchant houses had engaged in commerce with Newfoundland, not just in underwriting the visiting fishery. They had dealt with agents and local merchants arising in St John's as the chief port of entry, the capital, and the defence base, while British centres in Atlantic trade from London to Clydeside had extended their links as well. And continued growth in the island's resident fishery had made St John's an increasing focus of Newfoundland mercantile life: a life still bound to British markets, supplies, and credit, but by a more typical, less rudimentary and unbridled form of external metropolitanism than that which had gone before. In effect, the Newfoundland urban centre was moving towards headship within this newer metropolitan pattern – and changing from a makeshift jumble of shanties, sheds, and fishing berths which had held but some 185 settled inhabitants in 1675 to a thriving town of more than 3700 residents by 1796.

Despite all these changes, hidebound mercantilism and engrained policy were remarkably slow to give way in the British metropolitan core itself. In London as late as 1789 the secretary of state, William Grenville, affirmed: 'Newfoundland is in no respect a British colony.' Indeed, it would stay under the Home Office as if it were some kind of homeland fishing ground. Thus it was not till 1817 that the island received a year-round governor, not till 1824 that it got full rights of private property and civil rule, and not till 1832 that it obtained representative government as an acknowledged British North American colony. The legacy of Newfoundland's own early form of external metropolitan rule was that strongly persistent. And so were the marks left by a lengthy opening age on this much-dominated Atlantic regional hinterland.

## 2

On the Atlantic mainland, the French occupation of Acadia showed both early parallels with and significant differences from the Newfoundland experience. The process began in the same way, with individual fishing visits, not purposeful metropolitan out-thrusts. In due course, French fishermen who moved westward beyond the rugged Avalon came to the Gulf of St Lawrence shores, to those of future Cape Breton and Prince Edward Islands, and to the continental coasts behind. At harbours they frequented there, however, fur trading came increasingly to displace the taking of cod. In Newfoundland native Beothuks were driven from the shores and even slaughtered by visiting crews who brutally treated them as petty fishing rivals and thieves. But on the mainland, native tribes more often had abundant furs to barter, supplied from the dense continental forests. Hence in these newer areas a valuable alternative resource became tied into transatlantic markets, one which could well lead Europeans inland from the coasts. And in Acadia, as the French came to term this maritime land area, fur as well as fish drew metropolitan commitments, leading to the settlement at Port Royal on the Bay of Fundy in 1605. That colonizing French venture was launched by a substantial chartered company, whose headquarters were in the major Norman port of Rouen, close to the Paris market, but whose merchant investors came also from other westward-dealing port towns such as St Malo and La Rochelle.

Yet the colony so founded was itself to be prey to metropolitan forces, because Acadia was an area of chronic contention between France and England in America. An English foray destroyed Port Royal in 1613. The settlement next placed there by the succeeding Anglo-Scotch Company left little more behind it than the name, Nova Scotia, after France had regained Acadia in 1632. Some additional French settlers were brought out by new proprietors, but an expedition from New England took Port Royal again in 1654 and Acadia stayed under English control to 1670. Back in French hands thereafter, it only slowly added farmlands to frontier fishing stations and fur trade posts. By 1693 there were only some one thousand Acadian colonists on diked tidal flats and fertile lowlands along the Bay of Fundy, governed from Port Royal as their garrison centre and entrepôt. And though these hinterland Acadians seemed to dwell in isolation from the world outside, in reality they lived constantly exposed to its play of power.

On the one side, their territory bordered the sea approaches to the inland St Lawrence empire of New France, vital to French metropolitan interests. On the other, it edged a powerful and expansive New England, whose shipping by the 1690s carried much of Acadia's external trade and whose fishing craft treated its waters as virtually their own hinterland to exploit. The next great round of Anglo-French wars brought home this fatefully exposed position. Port Royal fell to attack from

New England in 1690, was won back, but was lost again in 1710. By the peace of 1713 Acadia became once and for all Britain's Nova Scotia, although France retained Cape Breton and Prince Edward Island on the sea route to Canada and kept an indefinite hold in the interior wilds beyond the Nova Scotian peninsula, over the passage north by land. But further, since Newfoundland had been ceded to Britain, and Placentia perforce abandoned, France required a new fishing and naval base for its northwest Atlantic interests. Hence the grand and costly works of Louisbourg went up after 1720, set on the Cape Breton foreshore and flanking the main entry to the Gulf of St Lawrence.

Louisbourg was not only a giant stone stronghold three-quarters of a mile long with a well-protected harbour for French warships and fishing vessels. It also was a town of over 3000 in the 1740s, almost a Normandy seaport transplanted, which carried on a large fishery and a busy Atlantic commerce. Here, in effect, was a striking urban product of metropolitan purpose and investment applied to the overseas hinterland from Paris, and its very life span would be determined by external forces. In 1745 New England militia brought by the Royal Navy captured the citadel after a seven-week siege – only to see London give Louisbourg back to Paris in the stalemate peace of 1748, thanks to distant power balances in Europe and India. But in 1758 during the Seven Years' War, the heavily fortified base would fall again, to a massive British expedition of regulars and naval units, and this time it was to be demolished, the town abandoned; all in consequence of metropolitan action and decision.

Before then, however, Louisbourg, and the French threat it embodied, had greatly affected the life of a nominally British Nova Scotia. That frontier province had been British-ruled since 1713, but almost wholly populated by French Acadians, amounting to around 10,000 by the 1750s. Their British masters felt vulnerable themselves, especially with Louisbourg restored to France in 1748 and New England outraged by the return of a menace to its sea lanes and fisheries which it had spent blood and wealth to erase. Accordingly, London founded Halifax in 1749 as a garrison and naval base to meet its dangerous French Atlantic rival. Set in a superb harbour on Nova Scotia's ocean coast, not on the inner Fundy shore as Port Royal had been, Halifax was henceforth to be the provincial capital as well. The town was thus from the start a deliberate metropolitan creation, first occupied by 2500 colonists shipped from London, laid out on a grid plan within log defences, and soon graced by a handsome, clapboard Anglican church, St Paul's, which was brought partly in frame from Boston, New England's own emerging metropolis. Moreover, New England traders moved northward to this new urban outpost, launching its early commercial growth. And growth accelerated after war was renewed with France in 1755. Masses of troops, warships, and supply convoys gathered at Britain's new northwest Atlantic base, where a naval dockyard was established, and contractors to the forces or merchant shippers quickly built a booming business. Halifax was inherently dependent on the transatlantic power behind it, but as the chosen agent of that power, it gained steadily in its own hinterland significance.

The year 1755 also witnessed the tragic, bitter expulsion of the French Acadians, a sweeping act of external dominance which this self-contained and strongly rooted local population nevertheless could not withstand. In stern effect, it cleared the way for new settlement in Nova Scotia from outside. New England 'planters' took over former Acadian lands on into the 1760s while other migrants soon arrived as well: Yorkshire English, Highland Scots, German Protestants, and Irish Catholics. Even by 1767 Nova Scotia had more than 12,000 inhabitants, chiefly farmers and resident fishermen (with few French or Indian constituents left among them) in a community which was gradually surmounting frontier existence and which had had its own structure of representative government since 1758. Over the same time Halifax, the headship centre, did not rise much beyond 3000 once the stimulus of wartime was removed – until the American Revolution broke out in 1775. Nova Scotia's Yankee settlers were now caught in counterpulls; but at its capital, the weight of officialdom, imperial expenditures, and a garrison much reinforced as war proceeded kept the overseas metropolitan ties firm. More than that, Halifax boomed anew with war markets and privateering enterprises, or with government projects to improve its port facilities and defences, including major works on Citadel Hill above the town.

More generally, too, the Revolutionary War made fields of commerce that had formerly belonged to much stronger competitors in New England accessible to Nova Scotia merchants. Within the mercantilist trade laws of the British empire – from which New Englanders had forcibly removed themselves – Nova Scotian ships now strove to supply Britain's West Indies possessions with foodstuffs and timber products in exchange for sugar and rum. True, a still backward province could largely furnish just fish and rough lumber; other supplies still came from New England, illicitly, but virtually accepted as necessary. Nevertheless, Nova Scotian merchants and shippers (and certainly those of its chief port) did increasingly well in the West Indies trade. Hence Britain's loss of its former American colonies, accepted at the peace of 1783, seemed of less consequence to the Halifax business community than the fact that their own province had remained inside the British metropolitan structure of seapower, protected imperial trade, and tariff preferences. To say with Innis that the external workings of the American Revolution changed Nova Scotia 'from an outpost of New England to an outpost of Old England' may overstate the case; yet it does aptly suggest the place this hinterland domain had thus acquired within the overseas hegemony extended from London.

Another consequence of the Revolution, the Loyalist movement, added substance to Halifax as well as to Nova Scotia in general. Aside from those evacuees from Boston who had swelled and strained the wartime town, the postwar influx of Loyalists helped to raise its population almost to 5000 by 1791, while approximately 25,000 came to Nova Scotia overall. And though Halifax's growth slowed once more in peacetime, the new and lengthy French wars from 1793 to 1815 brought on another generation of bustling military and mercantile activity, to leave at its close a city of over 10,000 in a province of 80,000. Internal developments in Nova Scotia undoubtedly contributed to this expansion, which also occurred in fishing outports, shipbuilding centres, and lesser commercial towns around the province from Yarmouth to Pictou. Still, the prosperous West Indies merchants and leading wholesale houses clustered at Halifax – and the wealth accumulated there from privateering that went on to finance trade and banking owed a great deal to the influence of outside forces on this key strategic base, which had been given a happily rewarding role in the pattern of external metropolitanism.

The influx of Loyalists also created the province of New Brunswick, set off from Nova Scotia in 1784, as thousands of these migrants settled on the Bay of Fundy's far shore or up the long river valley of the St John. As a result, Fredericton was decreed into being as a capital up-river, to be New Brunswick's military and cultural headquarters as well, and at the river mouth the main Loyalist arrival camp was chartered in 1785 as Saint John, Canada's first incorporated city. This city erected by fiat from London declined, however, in its first three years from 3000 to 1000 as inhabitants moved on to take up inland farms. But then it began to grow as a port, not only to supply the settlement frontier developing up the valley beyond, but also to export ship's masts cut for British naval contracts in the tall, dense pineries that lined the river. Woodyards, shipping, and shipbuilding came to mark Saint John, particularly after 1809 when the far larger and more lucrative square-timber trade started its long ascent. The loss of vital Baltic wood supplies to Britain during the Napoleonic Wars had led to much increased British duties favouring colonial timber. These tariff preferences, effectively subsidies prescribed in London, drew bulky square-hewed beams from British North America to feed metropolitan markets across the ocean. The inward-reaching forest frontier of New Brunswick was one main result; another was the flourishing of Saint John as a major focus of lumber-shipping and shipbuilding. It already had over 4500 inhabitants by 1810. Fostered by the long-distance export trade in seemingly endless forest resources, the city was to outstrip Halifax in size through much of nineteenth century. In short, one could hazard that no urban centre rising in an opening Atlantic Canada came more plainly to prosper by virtue of external metropolitan decision and dominance.

## 3

Charlottetown in its Prince Edward Island province of fishing, farming, and great estates of absentee land-owners might provide a further Atlantic model; but the demands of time and space must take us on to the St Lawrence. Jacques Cartier's voyages of 1534 and 1535 had early established France's claim to that waterway deep into the continent. French fishermen had advanced to harbours on the lower St Lawrence; Tadoussac had developed farther up as a meeting place for fur trading with the Indians. Yet no enduring French St Lawrence colony began until 1608, when Samuel de Champlain went still further up-stream to plant Quebec beneath the heights of Cape Diamond, there commanding narrows in the river, and so enabling fur monopolists to forestall 'interlopers' – the due word for unauthorized traders. Quebec, that is, was another product of metropolitan business enterprise, founded by the same chartered group that had begun Port Royal, which now sought to employ its trade monopoly on a great route to the resources of the interior.

Thus Champlain set up his little base, as the company's lieutenant 'in the country of New France.' Thus, in following years, he made his monumental journeys up-river to Lake Champlain, to the Ottawa and the Great Lakes, forging essential trade alliances with the tribes that would bring furs down to Quebec which remained a company entrepôt, serving metropolitan markets and investors by forwarding the yields from the St Lawrence hinterland. The first farm settler did not arrive at Quebec until 1617. There were only about seventy inhabitants in this capital of New France by 1628 before a seaborne English assault took and held it till 1632. Yet in that time, the distant Huron Confederacy between Lakes Huron and Ontario had been linked into the French trade, and as tribes beyond these vital middlemen also furnished them beaver in exchange for French goods, the fur traffic reached out to areas not yet seen by Europeans. In effect, the continent's broad central lakelands were increasingly drawn into an external metropolitan system that was funnelled out the St Lawrence and over the Atlantic. All this, moreover, before there was a real settlement frontier, or more than the tiniest urban nucleus in New France.

On that domain's return to French control in 1632, some effort to bring it settlers was made by the Company of One Hundred Associates, a more powerful, Paris-centred body which had succeeded to the trade monopoly and rights of governance. Seigneuries, too, were granted, and the advance post of Trois-Rivières established well above Quebec. By 1645 there were around 300 in the whole Laurentian colony, still the merest handful amid a vast fur trade hinterland. By then, however, another metropolitan factor besides the chartered company was also strongly in play – the religious thrust of the Counter-Reformation from a zealously Catholic France. One particular expression of this outreach was the mission of Ville-Marie founded in 1642 at the site of Montreal. It lay far up-river on the junction of the main native travel paths, and so was readily exposed to Indian attack, but equally placed to prove a most valuable fur trade site. More generally as well, religious impetus from the metropolitan core brought the Jesuits to serve in New France, whether at Quebec or in the wilds of Huronia. In any event, these dedicated venturers were not of the frontiers where they laboured, but were highly educated and disciplined churchmen from outside subject directly to the papacy in the clerical metropolis of Rome. Indeed, they conveyed a metropolitanism of Catholic faith, centrally organized and dominated, whose influence over the St Lawrence hinterlands would long outlast the brief Jesuit missions to the Hurons destroyed by 1650 during the ravages of war with the formidable League of the Iroquois.

The devastating Huron-Iroquois struggle itself displayed the workings of rival external metropolitan structures. The Huron and Algonkian allies of the French brought furs by way of the Lakes and the Ottawa to the St Lawrence link with France. The Iroquois Five Nations to the south of Lake Ontario were tied instead to Dutch traders on the Hudson and sought to divert or break the flow of furs eastward to Quebec. Hostility between the tribal groups was nothing new, but their mounting dependence on trade goods, virtually for survival, added desperate force to their conflict. Metropolitan traffic and technology had invaded and disrupted native life. And so the fighting that went on into the 1660s shattered the Hurons and other tribes in the Ontario peninsula between the upper and lower Great Lakes, while Iroquois war parties raided widely from Montreal to below Quebec.

Harshly strained, fur supplies all but cut off, the company regime in New France became practically paralysed. It was the central influence and strong finances of the metropolitan Jesuit Order that did much to keep the colony going. Then, finally, in 1663 another metropolitan agency, the powerful absolute state arising in France under Louis XIV, intervened to replace company rule with direct royal government. Governing officials tied closely to the developing bureaucracy in Paris took charge. Over 1000 regular troops were sent out to deal with Iroquois, leading to the peace achieved in 1667. And new militia organization, new civil machinery – but above all, new settlement – marked the active interposition of the metropolitan state on the St Lawrence.

Between 1663 and 1673 the population of New France tripled, from 2500 to over 7500, as the Paris authorities dispatched families of settlers, marriageable young women, indentured labourers, and masses of equipment in a deliberate design to make the colony both more self-sustaining and a market for French metropolitan goods other than fur trade supplies. Seigneurs acting as land agents settled arriving immigrants on their estates, thus expanding farm production and building rural markets for incipient towns. The able intendant, Jean Talon, not only supervised the work of settlement, but also pursued prospects of diversification in weaving, brewing, and tanning and lumbering, mining, and shipbuilding. His success was mixed, and French Canada remained basically dependent on its fur trade. Yet it did gain substantial agrarian underpinnings: the farm frontier now thrived along the mid-St Lawrence Valley. Though immigration dwindled after 1673, as the attention of the French state turned to wars in Europe, a robust rate of natural increase kept the French-Canadian populace growing. By then, in short, external metropolitanism had already done much to implant this hinterland community firmly in the St Lawrence region.

The consolidation of New France led on to a vast expansion in its fur hinterlands, beyond Lake Superior to the north, and south from the Great Lakes basin into the Mississippi Valley. At the same time another huge fur trade realm took gradual form above the French northern flank: a realm held by the Hudson's Bay Company, the powerful joint-stock company that was chartered in London in 1670 with title, fur monopoly, and governing rights in the English-claimed territories around the great Bay. The next year, as French emissaries at Sault Ste Marie proclaimed their own possession of the lands of tribes to the westward, the first Hudson's Bay cargoes went out to England from the Bottom of the Bay (James Bay). And by 1682, when that insatiable entrepreneur, the Sieur de La Salle, extended the reach of France to the mouth of the Mississippi, rival English and French fur trade expeditions faced one another far to the north, at the entrance to the Nelson River beyond the Bay. Again competing external metropolitan designs were to clash in North America, even this deep in the continental interior. The French sought to drive the English from remote, bleak northern shores, while far to the forested south the Iroquois, now allied with other English who had supplanted the Dutch on the Hudson River, launched new forays to break the inland trade lines to the French-held St Lawrence. The ensuing conflicts from the late 1680s on were bloody projections of metropolitanism overseas; as such, they were finally to be decided in Europe. At the peace of 1713 France had to recognize Britain's title to the Hudson Bay territories, even though in the hinterland warfare French forces had swept the Bay. On the other hand, the Iroquois had been crushed as an indigenous military power, and the western empire of New France preserved.

In the era of peace that followed, in general stretching from 1713 to mid-century, the settled French Laurentian colony matured very significantly. By 1754 its total population stood at 55,000, with Quebec, Montreal, and Trois-Rivières containing 8000, 4000, and 800 inhabitants, respectively. Of the two chief urban centres, the once-embattled outpost of Montreal swelled as the focus of the farspread St Lawrence fur trade, a headquarters for its powerful merchants as well as for voyageurs, artisans, and local storekeepers – not to mention the prominent Sulpician Order which actually held the Island of Montreal *en seigneurie*. The erstwhile little entrepôt of Quebec developed still more fully as headship city for the whole Laurentian region under French metropolitan dominance: the seat of its political and military command, of the Catholic church's religious and social authority, and of the mainline services in New France's commerce and transport overseas. Moreover, a compactly settled countryside appeared along the banks of the St Lawrence, integrated with its local marketing and administrative centres but maintaining a distinctive rural life under the institutions of seigneurialism. That life was to be enduringly distinctive; for the seigneurialism that had been transferred from the French metropolitan core community was modified in the Canadian hinterland – by a North American abundance of land, which made substantial habitants anything but downtrodden peasants, and by the necessary structure of militia service and the strength of military tradition in the French-Canadian community. This was assuredly a new regional society, emerging out of the seventeenth-century Laurentian farm frontier and well established before the decisive Seven Years' War handed French Canada over to British external metropolitan control.

In the half-century preceding that drastic upheaval, the French fur frontier saw changes of its own. It penetrated the great plains and forests of the northwest beyond the Lakes, far outdistancing its Hudson's Bay competitors on the one flank and the vanguard of traders pushing over the Appalachians from the British seaboard colonies on the other. French posts had advanced west to the Red and Assiniboine rivers by 1738, on to The Pas and the Saskatchewan by 1749. Yet this westward reach to fresh fur resources raised transport costs on ever-lengthening French travel routes and affected the very organization of trade. Canoe brigades now voyaged in regular patterns to specific posts while wealthy merchants in Montreal underwrote the operations and held the necessary government trading permits. The day of independent free-roving coureurs de bois was virtually over. The voyageurs who replaced them were no less tough and skilled but were paid employees contracted for the tasks of canoe transport by the funding bourgeoisie. Here, in fact, a large and complex metropolitan-hinterland traffic system was acquisitively at work. The need for a diplomatic and military presence to help maintain trade ties with Indian nations against British competition also sent French officers and garrisons to key inland posts. Indeed, the metropolitan regime in Paris came to supervise and support the forest trade for political and defensive reasons rather than for supply or profit. And that course led on to fort-building – then to the crucial contest for a continent.

Earlier in the 1750s the erection of French forts to hold the Ohio country soon brought British thrusts against them; armed encounters which merged in 1756 with the official onset of the Seven Years' War in Europe. Without going over that conflict in all its Canadian aspects, it bears recalling that the major critical battles were less frontier mêlées waged from behind trees than full-scale army-navy actions like the siege of fortress Louisbourg in 1758 or the set-piece combat of regular forces on the Plains of Abraham outside Quebec in 1759. Moreover, it was Britain's command of the waters off Europe, far from the hinterland wilds, which reduced the flow of reinforcements for the French in America to a trickle while men and matériel streamed overseas to British armies. Again external metropolitan power worked momentously on Canada's history. Accordingly, the peace of 1763 left Paris a metropolis for little more than St Pierre and Miquelon in North America and gave the French-settled Laurentian realm into London's keeping, henceforth as the British province of Quebec.

This switch in ruling metropolises meant changes in economic as well as political existence for the St Lawrence society. Its major commerce abroad had largely been conducted by the agents of French metropolitan firms stationed in Canada. With the ties to France broken, these merchants departed. Their place, however, was increasingly filled over the 1760s by English-speaking entrepreneurs – coming either directly from Britain's mercantile core or via its American colonies – who forged new links with the demands, commodities, and finances of British metropolitanism. In Quebec City they well might be contractors to garrison or government, shipping merchants, or, in time, timber dealers and shipbuilders. In Montreal they might take up wholesaling and forwarding, but above all they entered into the fur trade, now that the huge St Lawrence commercial hinterland had been opened to them. Accordingly, they formed partnerships with French Canadians experienced in the inland traffic; the one side provided access to trade goods, credit, and markets in Britain, the other knowledge of the wilderness routes, the voyageur workforce, and the native peoples.

After 1768, when continued Indian unrest in the interior had been placated and restrictions on fur trading lifted, Montreal commerce surged anew into the western expanses. True, the American Revolution soon brought fresh strains and dangers, when Montreal itself was occupied by American invaders for a time in 1775–6 and Quebec was sharply besieged. Yet Quebec's walls withstood an ill-equipped frontier Yankee army until British naval power brought in more metropolitan troops to end the siege. Furthermore, the Revolution cut off American fur trade competitors from British sales and goods, while Britain's forts in the interior and strength at sea shielded the main St Lawrence lines of commerce. During the war Montreal's trade, in fact, expanded much farther into the northwestern wilds above the Lakes, leading to the creation of the powerful North West Company by 1784. Without doubt, that enterprise of the distant interior owed a great deal to the efficacy of the British external metropolitan system in which it lay.

In 1784 as well, the American Loyalists arrived in their numbers, clearing pioneer farms on the upper St Lawrence and lower Great Lakes beyond the established French-Canadian seigneurial holdings. Their swelling influx led further to the division of the existing province of Quebec into Upper and Lower Canada in

1791, the antecedents of present-day Ontario and Quebec. By that date Upper Canada in the Ontario lakelands as yet held only about 14,000 inhabitants, but Lower Canada, the essential Laurentian Quebec, contained over 160,000 settled residents, roughly four-fifths of them French-speaking. In this most populous British North American colony, the ancestral city of Quebec retained its headship and after 1800 would rise as the main St Lawrence timber port, soon benefiting, like Saint John in New Brunswick, from the new metropolitan preferential duties. Montreal, however, was not just a regional satellite centre within the British external sway. Its own trading dominance extended far beyond the Lower Canadian or Quebec region across Upper Canada (whose supply and export traffic it largely handled) to the western prairies and northern Athabaska forests – and in 1793 reached to the Pacific with Alexander Mackenzie of the North West Company.

Inland wintering traders, voyageurs, and Montreal partners together had won two-thirds of the Canadian fur trade for that major St Lawrence enterprise by 1795, much surpassing the older Hudson's Bay Company and in the process making Montreal veritably Canada's first trans-regional metropolis. This outreaching city soon grew larger than the Lower Canadian provincial capital, Quebec: Montreal's own population mounted from 9000 in 1800 to 16,000 by 1816, surpassing the governing seat's 15,000. But while the initial emergence of Canada's own metropolitan centres thus seems to be especially exemplified by Montreal, one cannot forget that this city had developed within frameworks of external metropolitanism thrusting out of France or Britain. Hence, as the nineteenth-century urban system took shape in the Canadian regions now rising from frontiers, it did so after some two centuries of powerful metropolitan linkages from outside, from over the Atlantic.

4

The much less occupied areas of Canada farther west may be more briefly treated in this period of beginnings, always recognizing that external metropolitanism could affect them also. In the Ontario lakeland region, although a farm frontier of settlement scarcely existed there before the Loyalists came, French metropolitan lines of commerce had strongly operated since at least the mid-seventeenth century. Moreover, French posts placed at strategic sites on fur trade routes anticipated towns that appeared when subsequent land settlement spread; for example, Fort Frontenac where Lake Ontario and the St Lawrence met, or Niagara by the crossing of main east-west and north-south travel paths, or Toronto at the entry to a long-used passage northward from Lake Ontario to the Upper Lakes. Fort Frontenac was precursor to the Loyalists' Kingston, the first real town in Upper Canada, funnelling traffic to and from Montreal. The up-river province's capital was initially established at Niagara. But this was soon deemed too exposed to American attack and the government was moved to the new town of York, founded on Toronto bay in 1793. Patently, being deep in Great Lakes forests did not prevent basic developments and metropolitan decisions affecting the whole future course of Ontario regional growth.

By the time of the War of 1812, Upper Canada's population of Loyalists, post-Loyalist American pioneers, and lesser elements from Britain had grown close to

90,000. After 1815, when war had ended, the tide of British transatlantic emigration began to climb, enlarging and filling in the Upper Canada land frontier. We need not continue past 1815, however; merely note that by that time Kingston had around 2000 residents, if York only some 700. Yet the smaller community, the village provincial capital, was really already advancing to urban prominence under British metropolitan authority. It had its imperial garrison and government officialdom and their valuable markets to draw farm settlers to its vicinity, while military purposes and government contracts built its highways that tapped interior rural settlements and so extended the commercial hinterland of York's merchants. Hence from around 1812, at the very least, this little place was heading towards ascendancy in the Ontario region – set on a course which made it Upper Canada's first incorporated city, Toronto, in 1834 with over 9000 inhabitants. And that essentially came about through external, not local, determinations.

The huge unsettled western regions that lay beyond remained fur trade territories, even if, by 1812, a small, primal agricultural frontier was being opened in the Red River Valley by Lord Selkirk's settlers, then arriving from Britain via Hudson Bay. But the fur frontier held dominion over all; or rather, two great invading fur trade rivals had come to contend for dominance in the Plains West. From the northern coasts the Hudson's Bay Company had projected its London-based metropolitanism into mid-continent ever since erecting its first inland post, Cumberland House, on the lower Saskatchewan River in 1774. From the St Lawrence the North West Company had vigorously extended Montreal's own metropolitan system ever farther overland. The struggle of the companies, not ending until they were merged in 1821, certainly involved the transport advantages of the Bay's shorter sea route to the western interior. In any case, however, this was inherently a contest between two metropolitan instruments, each basically external to the west itself. Nor did wilderness conditions there or frontier episodes of violence obscure the crucial working out of far distant balances of strength. Although the Montreal company had reached much more widely through the west, with posts beyond the Rockies from 1807, its aggressive, flexible, yet loosely organized system was ultimately to be outmatched by the permanence and solid capitalization of the London joint-stock enterprise. And further metropolitan factors, such as access to financial and political power groups in ruling London, lay behind the final settlement that placed the Plains and Pacific Wests in the hands of the Hudson's Bay Company after 1821: now combined with its former Montreal rival, yet a London-centred metropolitan instrument still.

One might again note that North West or Hudson's Bay trading posts also were often predecessors of the towns and cities that later rose with western settlement, from Winnipeg outside Fort Garry to Edmonton, Kamloops, or Victoria. And while Vancouver did not have such an origin, its future site was uncovered by another metropolitan agency – the Royal Navy – when Captain George Vancouver's voyage of 1793 to chart the north Pacific coast disclosed the superb natural harbour of Burrard Inlet. No doubt, the Pacific West in itself remained but barely entered by the opening nineteenth century. Even in that primeval vastness, however, the intrusions of external metropolitanism by then had set compelling frontier marks.

At this point, our discussions having swept so broadly across regions and centuries, only a few general comments remain to be made. First (to remind us of inevitable complexities) metropolitanism, whether internal or external, as we have viewed it deals with mutual relationships not separate existences, and with spheres related to spheres not simply with specific, delimited urban centres or precisely defined territories. That much should be apparent from the whole foregoing wide-ranging discourse. Second, there is not – nor was intended – some uniform model of metropolitanism to be applied throughout. Instead of model-building, my aim was has rather been to discern and assess some of the varied, but altogether evident and numerous, metropolitan examples that run through the earlier phases of Canadian history. But third, one also can see in them common factors repeatedly present in Canada's long opening experiences with external metropolitanism. They include: the overseas thrusts from core communities that pushed resource frontiers and raised up regions (with often scant altruistic intent and sometimes at much cost); the pervasive fact of metropolitan power and organization, functioning in seemingly native wilds; the importance of long-range transportation, centred on the far metropolis; the significance of metropolitan political decision, finances, markets, and supplies; and the influence of ethnic, socio-cultural, and technological contributions from the core – to which the breadth of the topic in hand has often allowed but passing reference. By way of adding to that reference now, I might briefly recall that metropolitan culture *cum* technology built and characterized the stately churches of Quebec, planned and fortified commanding Louisbourg and Halifax, provided the vital means of transatlantic communications, and, for the wide interior, developed native canoe techniques into an extraordinary continental transport system.

Finally, it must be stressed that all that has been presented here on early external metropolitanism can itself only constitute an opening, or prelude, to the subsequent much greater growth of metropolitan centres and systems inside Canada, roughly from 1815 forward, although that is not a magic number. To go further, a good deal of what has been offered previously, in my first three lectures, would also obviously gain very much in demonstration or corroboration through closer looks at Canadian cities and regions in the particularities of their growth after 1815. But, as one eminent metropolitan spokesman, Rudyard Kipling, indeed has said – that is another story.